Art Deco
Sculpture and Metalware

Alfred W. Edward

Schiffer Publishing Ltd

77 Lower Valley Road, Atglen, PA 19310

Without the support (both physical and emotional) of my wife Linda, this book would not have been possible. It was Linda who wrote the notes, who urged me on, who supported me when I needed it. It was Linda who helped with the photos, and who typed, proofread, advised, and guided. It was Linda who believed in me—and I am grateful.

I am also grateful to the antique trade, which enthusiastically provided all the information and the merchandise available in this guide

Copyright© 1996 Alfred W. Edward

Printed in China
ISBN: 0-88740-994-6

Library of Congress Cataloging-in-Publication Data

Edward, Alfred W.
    Art deco sculpture and metalware/by Alfred W.
Edward.
       p. cm.
    Includes bibliographical references and index.
    ISBN 0-88740-994-6 (hard cover)
    1. Sculpture. Modern--20th century--Catalogs. 2. Art
Metal-work--History--20th century--Catalogs. 3. Art
deco--Catalogs. I. Title.
NK6410.E35 1996
735'.230412--dc20   96-19144
                                      CIP

Published by Schiffer Publishing Ltd.
77 Lower Valley Road
Atglen, PA 19310
Telephone: (610) 593-1777
Fax: (610) 593-2002

Please write for a free catalog.
This book may be purchased from the
publisher. Please include $2.95 postage.
Try your bookstore first.

We are interested in hearing from authors with
book ideas on related subjects.

Contents

Acknowledgements - 4

An Introduction To Art Deco - 5

Chapter 1: Early influences - 7
    C. R. MACINTOSH - 7
    VIENNA AROUND 1900 - 9
    OTTO WAGNER - 9
    JOSEPH HOFFMANN - 10
    THE WIENER WERKSTÄTTE - 12
    PERIODICALS - 13

Chapter 2: Austria - 14
    HAGENAUER - 14
    RENA ROSENTHAL - 67
    BALLER AND BOSSE - 75

Chapter 3: Germany - 81
    WMF - 81
    DEUTCHER WERKBUND - 91
    BAUHAUS - 92
    FERDINAND PREISS - 102

Chapter 4: France - 104
    CHIPARUS, PUIFORCAT & OTHER
      FRENCH ARTISTS - 104
    CONSTANTIN BRANCUSI - 106
    EDGAR BRANDT - 107
    BRONZE STATUARY - 108

Chapter 5: Denmark - 119
    GEORG JENSEN - 119

Chapter 6: Reproductions - 132

Chapter 7: On Collecting - 138

Bibliography - 140

Value Guide - 141

Index - 143

Acknowledgments

I would like to thank the many dealers, collectors, and auction houses that provided information, made items available for photography, or provided photographs for this book—particularly Christie's, New York; Barry S. Slosberg, Inc., Philadelphia; Hesse Galleries, Otega, NY; Dawson's Auctioneers, Morris Plains, NJ; The Auction Room Ltd., Forest Hills, NY; and also Savage Mills, Soren Jensen, Richard Bell, Sandra Chadwick, Richard Farber, Jr., Evelyn Gordon, Gloria Dunetz-Montage, Thomas Marone, Jeff Seck, Richard Wright, Glen Leroux, Howard Byer, Jeffrey & Coco, Bruce Horton, Paul Chmielewski, Francesco Johnson, Rosemary Schickler, Jacqueline Barratt, Catherine McCarthy, Katheleen Nye, Paul Kenyon, Stephen Leblanc, Renata Ramsburg, Stephen Lapidus, Janet Lehrer, Curt Braman, Jack Papadinis, George Creswell, David Roth, John Gascher, The Drawing Room of Newport, Ed & Helen Tobin, Mike Westman, Marjorie Levett, James Infante, Harriet Rossouw, Betty Ungar, Jack Swartz, Thomas W. Matarese, David James, Sandra Moran, Lon Manning, Rogers Ellingsworth, Lee Hargrave, Greg Weiss, Sal & Deborah Silvestro, Dennis L. Hancin, John Paul, Susan Collins, and a number of dealers who did not want to be mentioned. These dedicated professionals were a rich source of information otherwise unattainable.

I would also like to thank my son Eric Edward, whose artistic talent created the illustrations for this reference work

Introduction

The metalwares illustrated and discussed in this guide are a permanent record of the changing styles and concepts surrounding the Art Deco era. Beginning around the turn of the century in Europe, design went through many bold changes, from the over-ornamented and heavily decorated floral patterns of Art Nouveau to clean, geometric lines, using the square and the pierced square as a focal point. These changes affected the metalware made for everyday use, including furnishings (such as mirrors, candle holders, and smoking accessories), holloware, flatware, and decorative accessories. New manufacturing techniques evolved to accomplish these changes, and a new appreciation for handwork became apparent. The use of less expensive metals like brass, bronze and copper, and the use of plated goods enabled manufacturers and craftsmen to reach a broader market. Mass production of metalware for the common man began to receive more emphasis.

This pictorial value guide illustrates these dramatic changes. Included are the styles and designs of European Art Deco metalware available today, particularly items from well-known makers and workshops like Georg Jensen, WMF, Bauhaus, the Wiener Werkstätte and a number of French metalware manufacturers. In addition, I hope to fit the under-appreciated Austrian firm of Hagenauer into its proper place in the history of art, manufacturing, design, and collectibles, and to stimulate interest and inspire further research into this easily recognized manufacturing family.

When I began research for this project, the first thing I noticed was how much information is missing from the current publications. While a complete guide would be impossible to create, this book is intended to fill some of those voids. It will help you to understand the metalware manufacturing process and to recognize that the process is an art in itself, with the metalworker as the artist. Antique dealers, likewise, are the art historians. The histories of the firms discussed will indicate the success of the concepts of 'The Modern Trend' as it was envisioned by its founders.

All of the items illustrated were collected though the antique marketplace and represent the full range of material available. Most of the data in this book came from reliable and multiple sources. Some information can be gained from the merchandise itself. Catalogs and documents would help and this author is actively seeking them.

As part of my research I tried to reach the European antique market, with less than successful results; however, this sampling does represent the major northeast markets of the United States, with values for items available at the time of publication.

Chronology

In general, this book is organized in a chronological order; remember, however, that the manufacturers and designers were working simultaneously and individually all over Europe. The concepts and trends that they employed were shared through publications of the day, which will be mentioned elsewhere.

Chapter 1:
Early Influences

The Art Deco design concept, called the 'Modern Trend' in Vienna, had its roots in several areas of Europe. The end of the nineteenth century was a restless time for artists and craftsmen, and they needed a change of direction. An eager group awaited inspiration, and when it came their were a variety of leaders. Among them were Charles Rennie Macintosh, Otto Wagner, Josef Hoffmann, and schools like the Weiner Werkstätte.

Charles Rennie Macintosh (1868-1928)

An illustration of a chair designed by Charles Rennie Macintosh before the turn of the twentieth century. In 1995, this chair is still futuristic; indeed, it has been used repeatedly as a stage prop in the popular television show "Star Trek," set in the twenty-fourth century. *Illustration courtesy of Eric Edward.*

A 24"-long hand-hammered copper candle holder. This unmarked example shows the influence of Charles Rennie Macintosh. Au*thor's collection.*

Charles Rennie Macintosh worked primarily as an architect and interior designer in Glasgow, Scotland, and did very little metalwork. However, it is important to note his contribution to the Art Deco movement—not so much in design but in the ideal that made it possible. His early association with Viennese artists and craftsmen (Hoffmann, Olbricht, etc.) helped to define the style.

Macintosh worked with associates Herbert MacNair and the MacDonald sisters, Margaret (later Macintosh) and Francis (later MacNair), around 1895 to 1902. They were known in Glasgow as "The Four." They created highly stylized linear patterns adaptable to repoussé metal, gesso, and stained glass.

They produced candle sconces, mirror frames, clock faces, and panels often used in Macintosh's unorthodox furniture. Although most of his designs were transitional, the use of geometric shapes (particularly the square) predominates his work. The first pieces entirely free of Art Noveau-style were created in 1895. After this time his style experienced marked changes, reaching full maturity at the turn of the century.

The Four were invited to exhibit at the eighth annual Vienna Secessionist Exhibition in 1900, after which they exhibited in Munich, Dresden, and Budapest. Macintosh was asked to design a music salon for Frits Warndörfer, one of the founders of the Wiener Werkstätte, and in 1902 they exhibited furniture and decorative accessories in Turin, Italy.

Vienna Around 1900

In 1898, the inspiration for change and the Modern Trend started in Vienna, the 'Cradle of Modernism'. The concepts of Art Deco relied on the idea that the art world had to make its own future, and on a conscious effort to recognize the craftsman as artist and the artist as craftsman. It was an ideal of total art and a concern for working conditions that created these changes; the record will indicate that it was partly successful.

Otto Wagner (1841-1918)

Otto Wagner's contribution to the movement was primarily as a teacher. In 1894 he was appointed Director of Vienna's Academy of Fine Arts. His first address, entitled "Modern Architecture," was not well-received. Wagner felt that architecture should reflect the needs of modern civilization; that building should flow naturally rather than being predetermined or applied, and that appropriate materials should be used. This approach did not sit well with his old-school colleagues, but did gain favor amongst the proponents of the Modern Trend. As a teacher, he was superb and very influential. He selected his students with great care. His standards were demanding and he removed many less talented students from his program so that he could concentrate on the few most gifted ones. Under his tutelage, J.M. Olbrich, Josef Hoffmann, and many others became leaders of the new Modern movement.

Josef Hoffmann (1870-1956)

Josef Hoffmann was the undisputed leader of twentieth-century design in Vienna, and probably the world. He exerted a powerful influence on modern design in his day and well after his passing in 1956. As an architect and teacher his influence affected interior design, furniture, furnishings, and the applied arts. His metalware designs (though near impossible to find on the U.S. market today) are still highly sought-after by collectors and museums alike, commanding high prices at auctions.

Hoffmann arrived in Austria from Purnitz, Moravia in 1892 to study architecture at the Academy of Fine Art. As a 22-year-old student (one of the gifted students) he worked in the office of Otto Wagner. In 1898 he joined with Gustave Klimt and Koloman Moser to form the Vienna Secession, a collaborative of artists with no fixed program and no philosophy, concerned with traditional and secessionist (Art Nouveau) beliefs. These styles were both transitional and short-lived. Also in 1898 Hoffmann joined the School of Applied Arts and by 1899 was appointed as a professor.

During the Wiener Secessionist movement (as well as during the later Wiener Werkstätte days) Josef Hoffmann was a most prolific designer. His work was noted for its simplicity and functional beauty. The pieces were novel and yet logical, graceful and finely constructed. His first success was as a furniture designer and interior designer.

In 1900 he met Charles Rennie Macintosh while Macintosh was doing work for Frits Wärndorfer. Many experts felt that Josef Hoffmann modelled his work on that of Macintosh, but there is no evidence to support that. Even though their designs are similar, there are enough individual characteristics evident to disprove this theory. The evidence indicates that Macintosh and Hoffmann worked separately and independent of one another and, being motivated by like ideals, arrived at similar designs. It appears that Hoffmann's work, though similar, was better executed. It had a more practical style and was seldom eccentric. Hoffmann's furniture styles have stood the test of time, unlike Macintosh's.

Hoffmann succeeded Joseph Olbrich as artistic director of the School of Applied Arts. Art, like beauty, is in the eye of the beholder and Hoffmann's work was no exception. It was criticized fiercely by another of Hoffmann's contemporaries, architect Adolph Loos, who believed that "Tradition is everything—imagination is secondary." Branded by the secessionist as a non-artist, Loos initiated a compaign against ornamentation, with Hoffmann as his main target. Finally, however, Loos had to admit that Hoffmann's designs worked.

In 1903, Hoffmann and Koloman Moser, along with Gustave Klimt, founded the Wiener Werkstätte. Among Hoffmann's accomplishments were the founding of the Artists' Workshop in 1913, and his work as the chief architect for the Austrian Exhibit at the Paris Fair in 1925. He also helped develop low-income public housing in Vienna in the 1920s.

Many of Hoffmann's works through the years were purchased by the Museum of Applied Arts (MAK) in Vienna. Silver artifacts for the Wiener Werkstätte and a wooden jewelry box were the museum's first purchases. Thereafter, regularly sponsored surveys of products of the Wiener Werkstätte were conducted and many articles were bought. This merchandise, known as the travelling inventory, includes nearly 200 design drawings, as well as silver and brass objects executed by the Wiener Werkstätte. In 1947, MAK purchased the archives of the Wiener Werkstätte, including nearly 5000 drawings from every period of Hoffmann's work.

In 1960 Vienna rediscovered its own early twentieth-century artistic production. In 1964 the Historisches Museum der Stadt Wien laid the foundation for a general resurgence of interest in this period, following it with a major exhibit in 1967. Often throughout his career, Josef Hoffmann gave credit to Koloman Moser and Otto Wagner for their influence on his work.

An illustration of a silverplated white metal stepped ink stand, 3.5" x 3.5" x 4" tall. Designed by Josef Hoffmann and executed by the Wiener Werkstätte. *Courtesy of Eric Edward.*

An illustration of a 6.75"-diameter polished silver bowl in the openwork pattern "Arched Ivy." Designed by Josef Hoffmann and executed by the Wiener Werkstätte. *Courtesy of Eric Edward.*

An illustration of an eight-armed girandole in a hammered silver finish, 8.75" tall. Designed by Josef Hoffmann for the Wiener Werkstätte. *Courtesy of Eric Edward .*

The Wiener Werkstätte (1903-1931)

An illustration of a fan-shaped brass footed vase, 8.25" tall. Designed by Josef Hoffman and executed by the Wiener Werkstätte prior to 1918. *Courtesy of Eric Edward.*

The Wiener Werkestätte's concept of total artwork, including a mission to "revitalize culture," was aimed at the younger generation. The Wiener Werkstätte (or "Vienna Workshop") taught freedom of modern expression, and sought to achieve figural expression through functionalism and integrity in the use of materials. Their principal that "all art is good," that there is no difference between high art and low art, was a lofty ideal. In addition, the Wiener Werkstätte was a crafts collective, concerned about the working conditions of the artists and craftsman they were trying to unite.

As a school supported and endorsed by the museums, they were more concerned with patrons than with customers. According to some authorities, the Wiener Werkstätte was always in search of the kind of patron they referred to as a 'milk cow,' like their principal benefactor Frits Wärndorfer. Under his patronage, they achieved a high standard of design and manufacture. Their materials were selected for their cost, and only the most expensive materials were used. The designs, influenced by Charles Macintosh and the British Arts and Crafts movement, were generally geometric, with the pierced square dominating the motif. New styles, with good proportions and for useful purposes, were produced in their own workshop for sale to the trade and in department stores. The Wiener Werkstätte produced items in metalware, furnishings, furniture, interior design, fashion and ceramics, and were involved with architecture, publishing, and stage design. Despite this diversity, most of their production was purchased by their select patrons and by museums.

In 1905 the Weiner Werkstätte published a catalog and employed a hundred workers. In 1907 they distributed for Wiener Keramics. Also in 1907, Koloman Moser left the group to paint. In 1910 retail outlets played an important role in sales and in 1914, because of Austria's trade laws, the Werkstätte was given factory status. Over these years, the Wiener Werkstätte participated in a number of international exhibitions, including the following: 1908-1909 (Vienna), 1911 (Rome), 1914 (Cologne; sponsored by Deutcher Werkbund), 1916 (Sweden), 1917 (Switzerland), 1920 (Vienna), and 1925 (Paris). In 1921, International Style architect and designer Josef Urban opened a branch gallery of the Weiner Werkstätte in New York City.

An illustration of a fan-shaped silver footed vase, 8.25" tall. Designed by Dagobert Peche and executed by the Wiener Werkstätte in 1923. *Courtesy of Eric Edward.*

In spite of its near-perfect record of achievement, the Werkstätte was destined for failure. Through the years, the policy of producing one-of-a-kind items in expensive materials for the well-to-do led to the group's demise. Failure to industrialize and limited sales to common people, along with the squandering of resources in the name of art, also contributed to their downfall. In 1924 the New York gallery went out of business. In 1931 the Werkstätte itself went bankrupt, and sold all the remaining inventory in 1932.

Periodicals

Throughout the years of the Art Deco revolution, ideas were spread in many of the same ways they are today. Of particular importance at the turn of the century were periodicals. Many articles were written and new ideas were published in magazines and trade journals. Photographs and drawings were often used to illustrate styles and trends. At the turn of the twentieth century, there were several periodicals dedicated to the arts.

The magazine *Academic Architecture* was published from 1888 to 1897;

Deutsche Kunst und Dekoration and *Innendekoration* were published in German in the1890s.

Dekortive Kunst and *Dieskunst* were published in 1897 and 1899.

Ver Sacrum, the journal of the Wiener Werkstätte, published works of the Austrian school during their existence.

Art et Décoration and *L'art Décoratif* were published in French.

Bauhaus published their own journal, and in 1923 the magazine *Das Kunstblatt* was published.

The magazines *Arts and Architecture* and *Art and Design* were published in the United States from the1950s through 1980s and continuing through today the publication of periodicals plays an important role in design concepts and ideas.

Chapter 2

Austria

Austria, with Vienna as its cultural center, has produced some of the most important and well-known artists, craftsment and metalware manufacturers of the twentieth century. Firms like Hagenauer, Baller, Bosse and others produced decorative accessories and furnishings available for everyday use. Artists including Bruna Zach, Argentor, and Josef Lorenzl created bronze statuary for international trade. Many of these prominent craftsmen studied in other cities and sold their wares in other markets, as did Bauhaus student Karl Aubök. Research about these makers presents only a small sampling of clues, often in the form of the merchandise itself.

An illustration of a fan-shaped brass footed base, 8.25" tall. Designed and executed by Hagenauer; marked "WHW / Made in Austria." Note similarities to previous items. *Courtesy of Eric Edward.*

Hagenauer

The firm of Hagenauer began production of its own designs in 1898, when Carl Hagenauer (*1872-1928*) opened his workshop. They also produced some designs by Josef Hoffmann and the Wiener Werkstätte, as evidenced by items marked with both the Hagenauer touchmark and that of the outside designer.

As a contemporary of Josef Hoffmann, Carl Hagenauer's decision to join the Modern Trend was a wise one (as far as we're concerned). His impact on twentieth-century design was both important and inspirational. The Hagenauer products available now, at the turn of the twenty-first century, represent nearly one hundred years of quality in design and workmanship that is rarely equalled today.

Carl Hagenauer apprenticed as a goldsmith with the firm of Wurbel and Czokally, and served as journeyman goldsmith with Bernauer Samu of Pressburg, Austria (both prominent Austrian jewelry manufacturing firms).This experience in casting gold and silver in the lost wax technique became the basis for his own new venture. His early work, often described as Arts and Crafts by today's collectors, exhibits his mastery of these skills.

A 12"-diameter plate, hand-formed brass with a nickel-plated finish. Marked with the Hagenauer touchmark and "Made in Austria." This plate is an example of an Arts and Crafts design made by Carl Hagenauer. *Courtesy of David Roth.*

The bronze castings shown in the photographs here are fine examples of this very difficult process. His work in repoussé, as evidenced in these bookends, is quite remarkable.

Repoussé brass sheet-metal bookends with a polished finish, 6" tall. Marked with the WHW touchmark only. These bookends are a fine example of Carl's mastery of metalworking skills. Though not Art Deco, they indicate a transition from classical or historic design to a more modern style. *Courtesy of Jack Swartz.*

The machine- and hand-work involved in the manufacture of these pieces indicate the firm's apparent grasp of modern-day skills by any standards. Carl Hagenauer's early manufacturing capabilities and experience attracted a diversified market, including Hoffmann and the Wiener Werkstätte, Otto Prutcher and others. His products were available in leading department stores, as was the trend of the day.

The firm of Hagenauer exhibited its work and won awards for its designs in several major exhibits in Paris, London and Berlin. Thie firm's work was exported around the world. Very few of these early "Weiner Bronzewaren" items made by Carl are available on the antique market today, and are very desirable.

However, most pieces available today are still reasonably priced, only because they are less easily recognized by collectors. Early Hagenauer items (pre-1914) were generally marked with the word "Austria," or with the WHW touchmark and the word "Austria." The reference "Made in" was added by law in 1914 and had to be included on all items made for export; therefore, most items marked "Made in Austria" were made after 1914.

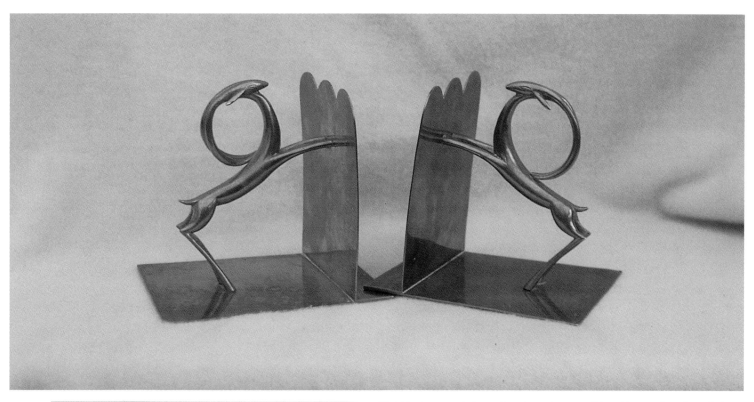

Cast bronze antelope bookends on polished brass sheet-metal bases, 5" tall. Marked with the WHW touchmark and made in Austria. *Courtesy of Jack Swartz.*

A 5"-tall cast bronze cigarette lighter in the form of a mouse, with a nickel-plated finish, on a spun brass base. Marked "Gimbel Austria" only. This piece is an early unmarked Hagenauer item made for sale by Gimbel. *Author's collection.*

17

A deer and fawn in cast yellow-colored bronze on a mahogany base, 26" long. Marked with the WHW touchmark. *Courtesy of Lon Manning.*

This 5"-tall antelope cigarette lighter is another example of
the early Hagenauer special-order items made for Gimbels.
It is nickel-plated cast bronze. *Author's collection*

Carl Hagenauer's influence on this family-operated metalware manufacturing business was the basis for the firm's continued success. His designs, influenced by his society, created the look we recognize as Hagenauer style today. Carl Hagenauer was the principal influence and sole proprietor of the Hagenauer workshop from 1898 until 1919 (when his son Karl joined the firm). He developed the manufacturing process and style of the firm, and established the standard for the quality and finish we recognize today. Carl Hagenauer studied with and from the masters, and should be recognized with them as a leader in twentieth-century design.

A 2"-tall cat with arched back in cast bronze with a black patina. Marked "WHW / Made in Austria." *Author's collection.*

A polished, cast bronze horse, 1.5" tall. Marked "WHW / Made in Austria." Another early animal form. *Author's collection.*

A polished, cast bronze bison measuring 2.5" and marked "WHW / Made in Austria." *Author's collection.*

A polished, cast bronze kangaroo, 3" tall, marked "Made in Austria" only. *Author's collection.*

A green-patinated bronze cast in the form of a dog, 2.5" high. Marked "WHW / Made in Austria." *Author's collection.*

A stylized cast bronze dog, 2.5" tall, with a black-colored and polished bronze-style finish. Marked "WHW / Made in Austria." *Author's Collection.*

A 2.5"-tall calf made of cast and polished bronze with an applied tail. Not marked. *Author's collection.*

A green-patinated pig dancing a jig, 3.5" high, cast in bronze. Marked "WHW / Made in Austria." *Author's collection.*

A 2"-tall whimsical cast elephant, black and bronze. Marked "WHW / Made in Austria." The 'black and bronze' style differs from black patination in that the patina is coated on the bronze material rather than being applied into it. *Author's collection.*

A 1.5"-tall comical cast black and bronze elephant. Marked "Made in Austria." *Courtesy of Gloria Dunetz-Montage.*

A male monkey holding an apple, polished cast bronze, black-patinated, 1.5" tall. Not marked. Black patination differs from 'black and bronze' style in that the patina is applied into the bronze material rather than coated on it. *Author's collection.*

A polished, cast bronze running mouse, 2" tall. Marked "WHW / Made in Austria." This piece is cast from the same mold as the item marked "Gimbel" shown earlier. *Author's collection.*

A stylized nickel-plated cast bronze figure in the form of a walking mouse, 3" tall. Marked "WHW / Made in Austria." *Author's collection.*

A 1.25"-tall seated cast dog, black and bronze, marked "WHW / Made in Austria." *Courtesy of George Cresswell of The Antiques Center at Historic Savage Mill.*

A cast, black-patinated cockerel, 2". Marked "WHW / Made in Austria." Note similarities to and differences from the cockerel shown previously. Variations in a given series can be quite extensive. *Author's collection.*

A cast, black-patinated crowing cockerel, 2.5"tall. Marked "WHW / Made in Austria." *Author's collection.*

A 'mate' to the two previously shown cockerels, 2" tall. *Author's collection.*

A whimsical 2.5"-tall skipping rabbit in cast bronze, with "Made in Austria" impressed on the top of the base. Often these post-World War II animals were marked with a ring tag attached to the leg, now often missing. *Author's collection.*

A cast squatting monkey, black and bronze, 2.5" tall. Marked "WHW / Made in Austria." *Author's collection.*

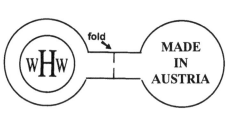

A ring tag

A cast, patinated figure in the form of terrier, 2.5". Marked "WHW / Made in Austria." This piece was manufactured for several years. Later examples are often not marked. *Author's collection.*

A cast, stylized kicking buffalo, 2" tall, black and bronze. Marked "WHW / Made in Austria." *Author's collection.*

A doe and fawn cast in black and bronze, 4" tall (doe) and 1.75" (fawn). The doe is marked "WHW" and "Made in Vienna Austria," an unusual mark for a small item. The fawn is not marked. *Courtesy of Jeffrey & Coco .*

A cast, black-patinated bronze playful goat, 5". Marked "Made in Austria WHW." *Author's collection.*

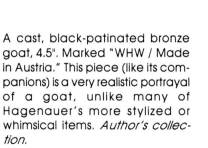

A cast, black-patinated bronze goat, 4.5". Marked "WHW / Made in Austria." This piece (like its companions) is a very realistic portrayal of a goat, unlike many of Hagenauer's more stylized or whimsical items. *Author's collection.*

A cast, black-patinated fawn, 4.5". Marked "WHW / Made in Austria." *Courtesy of Marjorie Levitt.*

Below:
A cast, black-patinated horse in a realistic style, 6" long. Marked "Made in Austria" only. This piece has an unusual hooped-shaped base. *Author's collection.*

A carved wooden antelope with cast, brown-patinated antlers, 14" tall. Marked "WHW / Made in Austria / Hagenauer Wien / Handmade." *Author's collection*.

A cast, black-patinated deer with brass-colored antlers, 7" long. Marked "WHW / Made in Austria / Hagenauer Wien / Handmade." This indicates that the piece was made after World War II. *Author's collection.*

A pair of stylized, carved wooden birds, 5" tall, with copper feet and multicolored inset wooden eyes. Marked "WHW / Made in Austria / Hagenauer Wien / Handmade." *Author's collection.*

A 7.5"-long carved wooden dachshund, marked "WHW / Made in Austria / Hagenauer Wien / Handmade." *Courtesy of Stephen Leblanc.*

Karl Hagenauer (1888-1956)

Under Karl's influence the firm of Hagenauer became more recognizable, since he expanded and popularized the company's styles. His studies (a degree in architecture) at Vienna's Kunstgewerbbeschule ("Arts and Crafts Institute") with Josef Hoffmann and Oscar Strnad further influenced his design choices. Under Karl's leadership, the firm continued to manufacture merchandise of ever-increasing quality. The manufacturing process evolved to include high-quality plating and sheet-metal manufacture. The style, once again, reflected the mood and attitude of the day. The Roaring Twenties were beginning to have an effect on design, evident in the firm's work.

Karl Hagenauer was 31 years old when he came to work in his father's workshop. It was just after the First World War and people had a fresh new attitude. The concepts of the Modern Trend were now one generation old, and starting to have their effects. Women were being seen in a whole new light—as displayed in photographs of the day, they were becoming more active, less inhibited, more avante garde and stylish. A new-found freedom was exhibited in the style of the day and it is evident in the merchandise. Play was once again important, and once again it was reflected in the styles.

Karl Hagenauer's contribution to the firm was as a sculptor. His work in silver, copper, bronze, ivory, enamel, wood, and stone often shows the influence of Josef Hoffmann and Wiener Werkstätte. He was awarded a gold medal for outstanding workmanship and style in Milan. He was an honorary member of the Austria Workunion and a member of the Austrian Workshop, both in Vienna. After his father's death in 1928, Karl (along with his sister Grete and brother Franz) continued to operate the firm. They opened a retail store and woodworking shop in Salzburg, as well as in Vienna, where only the highest quality merchandise was sold.

A 5"-tall cast black and bronze bust of a Nubian, marked "WHW / Made in Austria." *Courtesy of Greg Weiss and Diane Chichelli.*

Julius Jirasek (1896-1966)

It is the author's belief that Jirasek was the husband of Grete Hagenauer. Julius Jirasek studied at the Arts and Crafts Institute with Oscar Strnad, and received a degree in architecture. Machine and furniture design, industrial and interior design, metalware, and crafts were all taught in the architecture curriculum as part of the concept of "Total Art" discussed earlier. Like all youths of his age, Julius was called to duty during World War I. While in the military he was captured by the Russians, and during his captivity he developed an interest in ethnic art. He spent his time studying ethnographic artifacts in the Gobi desert and Ural. In 1923, upon his release, he returned to school and studied in the U.S.A. on a scholarship from the Workunion.

An ebonized, carved Nubian made of wood, on a turned brass base, 5" tall. Marked "WHW / Made in Austria / Hagenauer Wien / Handmade." *Author's collection.*

A cast, black-patinated Nubian woman, in a seated pose, 10" tall. Marked "WHW / Made in Austria / Hagenauer Wien / Handmade." *Courtesy of Lon Manning.*

Below:
A cast figure of a child sitting, black and bronze, 2.5" tall. Marked "WHW / Made in Austria." *Author's collection.*

A cast boy, black and bronze, on a turned and polished brass base, 4.5" tall. Marked "WHW / Made in Austria / Hagenauer Wien / Handmade." *Courtesy of Ed and Helen Tobin.*

A cast, black and bronze native boy who appears to be whistling, 3" tall. Marked "WHW / Made in Vienna Austria." *Author's collection.*

A cast boy, black and bronze, 2.5" tall. Marked "WHW / Made in Austria" *Courtesy of Paul Chmielewski.*

A cast, black-patinated whimsical warrior on a brass lion skin rug, 6" tall. Marked "WHW / Made in Austria / Hagenauer Wien / Handmade." *Author's collection.*

A cast, black and bronze baby crawling with a bronze hoop ring around it's neck, 2" tall. Marked "WHW / Made in Austria." *Author's collection.*

A cast, black-patinated bronze warrior with a polished brass shield and spear, 5.5" tall. Missing feather from head. Marked "WHW / Made in Austria." *Courtesy of Paul Chmielewski.*

A pair of cast, black-patinated warriors with polished brass spear and shield, 6" tall. Marked "WHW / Made in Austria / Hagenauer Wien / Handmade." *Courtesy of David James.*

A 6"-tall seated male warrior, cast, black-patinated, with a polished brass spear and shield marked "WHW / Made in Austria / Hagenauer Wien / Handmade." *Author's collection.*

Three cast, black-patinated bronze warriors, 6" tall, in a 9"-long carved mahogany canoe. Marked "WHW / Made in Austria / Hagenauer Wien / Handmade." *Author's Collection.*

A cast, black-patinated bronze warrior with a brass shield and spear, 6" tall. Marked "WHW / Made in Austria / Hagenauer Wien / Handmade." Courtesy *of Paul Chmielewski.*

A trio of black cast warriors ranging in size from 4.5" to 6", with brass feathers, shields, and spears. "Marked Made in Austria / Wein,/ WHW touchmark / Handmade." *Courtesy of It's Your Turn Antiques.*

A comical black-patinated warrior, 2.5". Marked "WHW / Made in Austria / Hagenauer Wein / Handmade." *Courtesy of Richard Bell.*

A cast, black and bronze native, 6" tall. Marked "WHW / Made in Austria / Hagenauer Wein / Handmade." Note the natural grass skirt. This piece is an outstanding example of Hagenauer's work from the post-World War II period. *Author's collection*.

Julius became an independent designer in Austria specializing in interior decoration, both commercial and residential. In 1930 he joined the firm of Hagenauer, where he produced silverware, silver jewelry, ceramics, lighting devices, glass, and furnishings. In 1951, he received an art award from the city of Vienna. Because of his particular interests, it is likely that he was responsible for Hagenauer's production of ethnographic art during the 1940-1950 period.

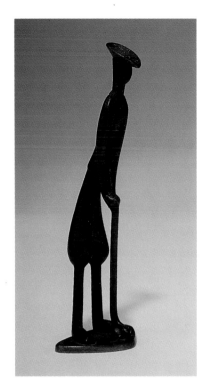

Franz Hagenauer (1906-1986)

Franz Hagenauer was the youngest son of Carl, and a brother to Karl. Even when he was twelve years old, his interest in the arts was apparent. He attended a course taught by Franz Cizek, given for youth at the Arts and Crafts Institute. As a fifteen-year-old he studied sculpture with Anton Hanak. In 1926, at age twenty, he joined his father's firm (during 1926, 1927, and 1928 all three Hagenauer men were active in the firm). He was a member of the Kunstschau (Art Show) and produced works in copper and bronze such as "The Christ of Innsbruck," a child's head exhibited in the Austrian Gallery, and a metalware emblem for the Vienna Parliament. He exhibited at the Biennale in Venice. In 1934, models for machines and tools to manufacture metal and wood were developed. At this exhibit, Franz received a prize from the city of Austria for applied arts.

A brown patinated golfer on a triangular stand, 3" tall. Marked "WHW / Made in Austria." This is another fine example of pre-World War II influence. *Author's collection.*

A green-patinated bronze female figure skater, 3" tall. Marked "WHW / Made in Austria." This classic Hagenauer piece is representative of Karl's early influence on the firm. *Author's collection.*

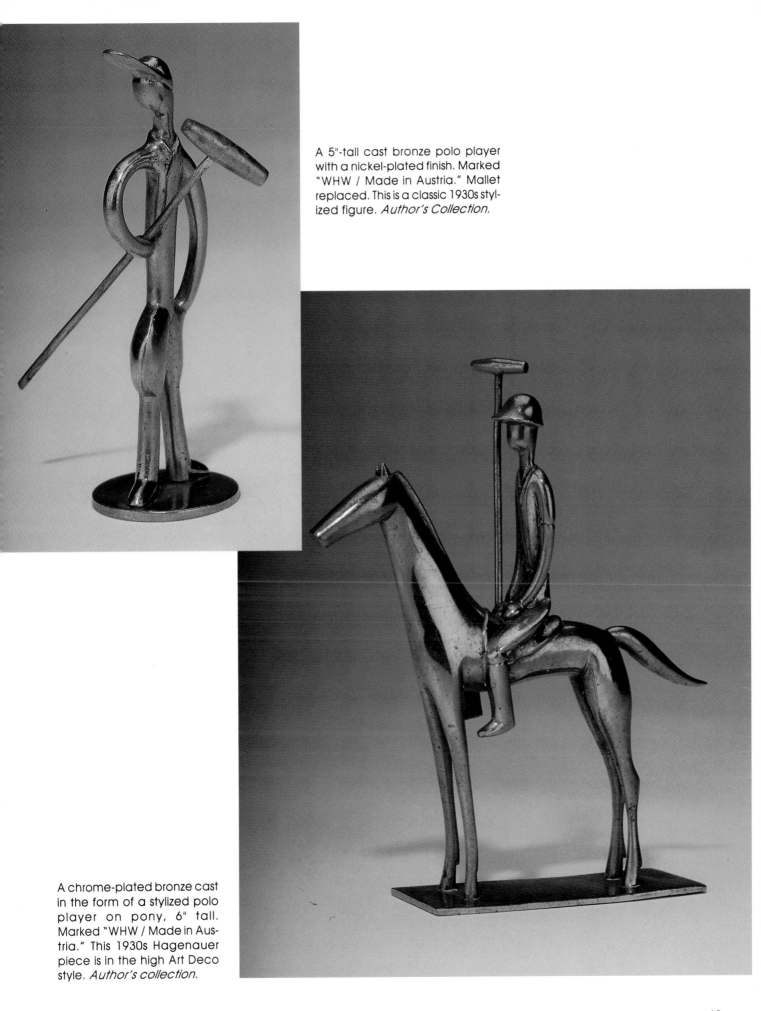

A 5"-tall cast bronze polo player with a nickel-plated finish. Marked "WHW / Made in Austria." Mallet replaced. This is a classic 1930s stylized figure. *Author's Collection.*

A chrome-plated bronze cast in the form of a stylized polo player on pony, 6" tall. Marked "WHW / Made in Austria." This 1930s Hagenauer piece is in the high Art Deco style. *Author's collection.*

41

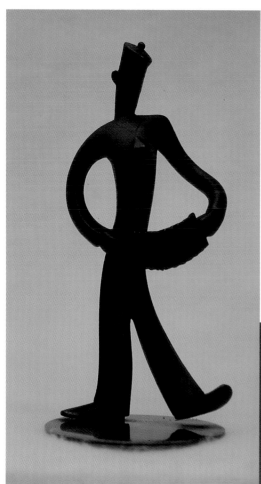

A 4.75" comical sailor playing the accordion. This is a cast black and bronze piece on a 3" circular polished bronze sheet-metal base. Marked "WHW / Made in Austria / Hagenauer Wien / Handmade." *Courtesy of Richard Bell.*

A chrome-plated cast bronze lady supporting a toothpick holder, 3.5". Marked "WHW / Made in Austria." Another example of the highly stylized 1930s motifs. *Author's collection.*

A 4.5" cast bronze figure on a polished cast bronze base, with polished brass rings around the neck. Marked "WHW / Made in Austria / Hagenauer Wien / Handmade." This bronze example **(compare to the photograph on page 32)** shows the use of a pantograph in translating designs from one medium to another. *Courtesy of Gloria Dunetz-Montage.*

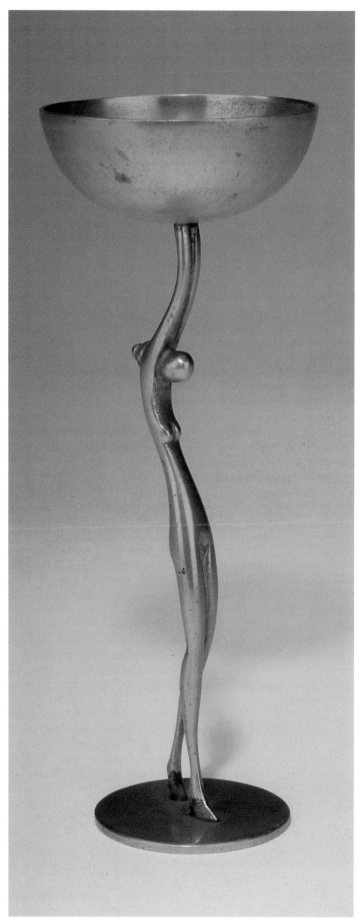

A nickel-plated cast bronze figure of a woman supporting a cup, 6" tall. Marked "WHW / Made in Austria." Another highly stylized 1930s piece. *Author's collection.*

Franz Hagenauer's influence on the designs of the Hagenauer firm was seen from the 1930s onward. Items manufactured from his designs, many identified with his mark, are commanding a great deal of interest and high prices on today's market. Franz's influence during the later years of Hagenauer Wien was substantial and he continued the family tradition of commitment to quality of design and manufacture. In 1962, Franz was appointed head of the master class in metal at the High School of Applied Arts. He passed away in 1986.

A cast bronze figural lamp of a stylized seated monkey gripping a tree trunk. 20.25" tall. Marked "WHW / Made in Austria." *Courtesy of Christie's, New York.*

A 15.25"-tall cast bronze figure of a bent arm holding a mirror. Unmarked. *Courtesy of Christie's, New York.*

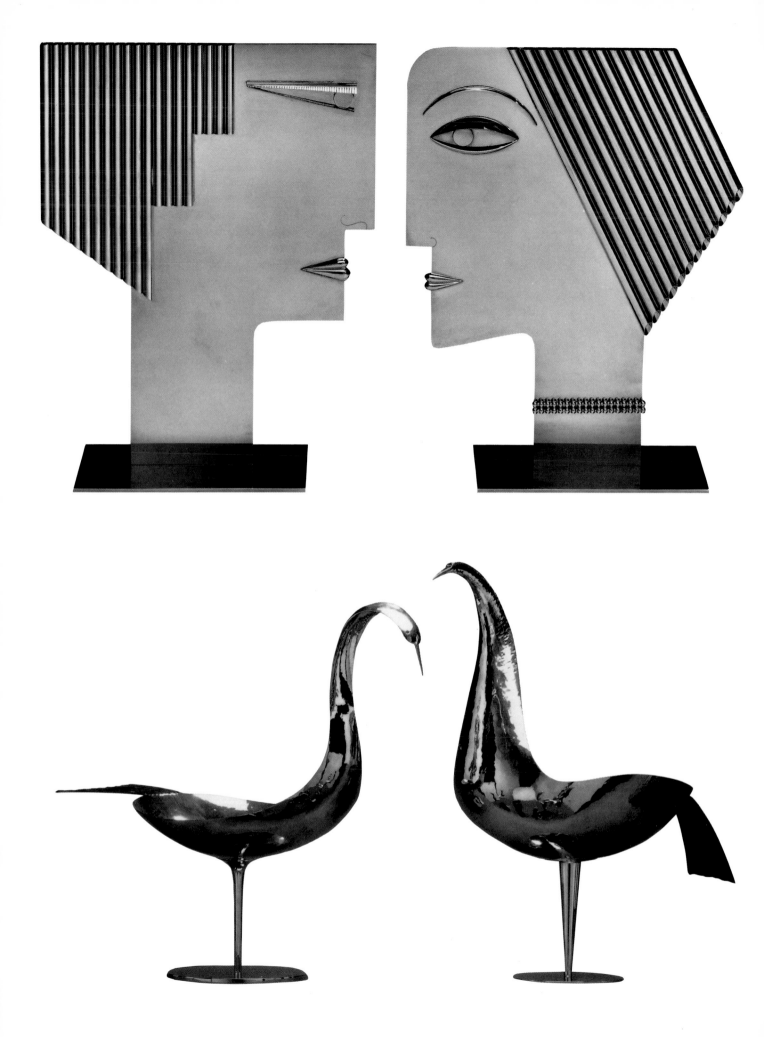

Opposite page, top:
A pair of 24"-tall stylized busts, formed as a male and female in profile, both with angular features. The applied haircuts are formed from hollow cylindrical tubes. Marked "WHW / Made in Austria / Hagenauer Wien." *Courtesy of Christie's, New York.*

Opposite page, bottom:
A pair of 16.25"-tall metal compotes, each formed as a stylized bird raised on a slender standard and circular foot, with a hammered finish. One marked "Franz / Hagenauer Wein / Made in Austria," the other marked "Hagenauer Wien / Made in Austria." Both stamped "WHW." *Courtesy of Christie's, New York.*

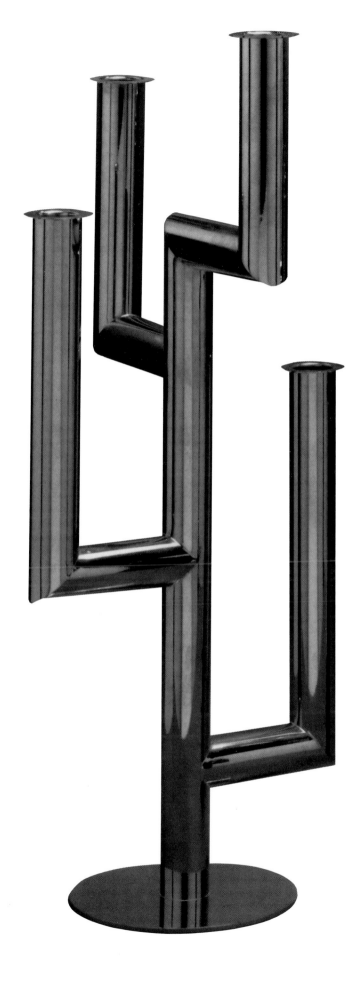

Right:
A 20.25"-tall four-armed metal candlestick supported on a circular foot with removable bobeches. Marked "Franz / Hagenauer Wien / Made in Austria." *Courtesy of Christie's, New York.*

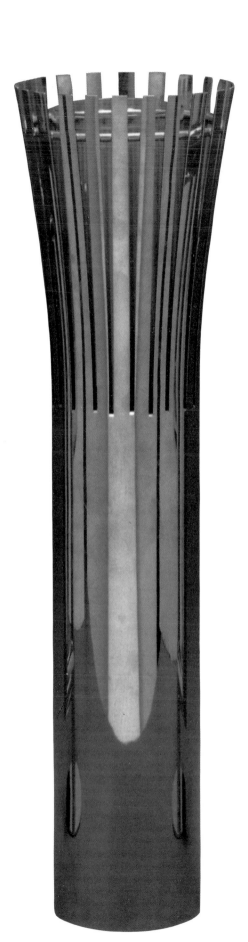

A cylindrical metal vase with pierced neck and glass liner, 16.25" tall. Marked "Franz / Hagenauer Wien / Made in Austria." *Courtesy of Christie's, New York.*

A stylized brass figural group in the form of a nude couple, 44" tall. Marked "WHW / Hagenauer Wien / Made in Austria." *Courtesy of Christie's, New York.*

A stylized brass bust in the form of a female with windblown hair, 25" tall. Marked "WHW / Hagenauer Wien / Made in Austria." *Courtesy of Christie's, New York.*

A chrome-plated metal bust in the form of a bare-breasted woman with elongated features, 19.25" tall. Marked "H Hagenauer / Wien Franz / WHW." This figure is a classic example of Hagenauer's repoussé skills. *Courtesy of Christie's, New York.*

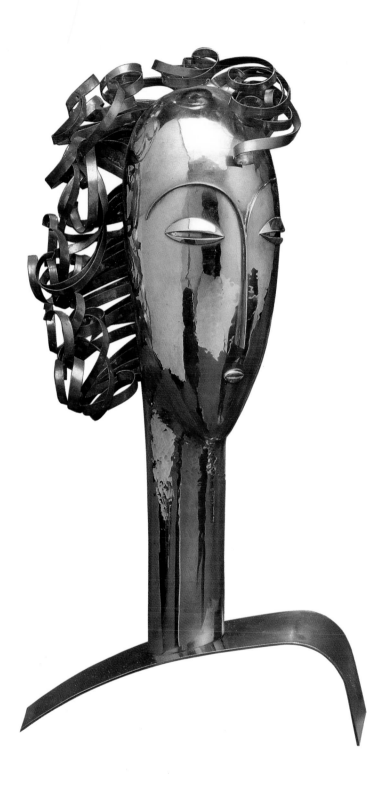

A stylized brass and copper bust of a serene young woman with curly hair, 20.25" tall. This sheet-metal sculpture is marked "Hagenauer Wien / WHW / Made in Austria." *Courtesy of Christie's, New York.*

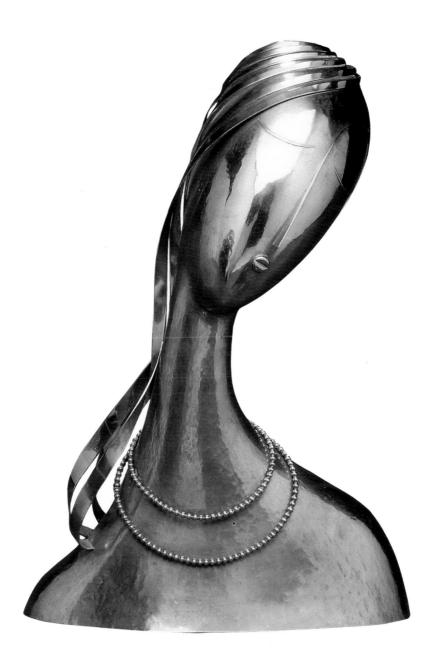

A stylized brass bust depicting a woman with long hair and a beaded necklace, with a hammered finish, 18" tall. Marked "Franz / Hagenauer Wien / Made in Austria / RB / WHW." *Courtesy Christie's, New York.*

Left: A stylized sheet-metal cardholder in the form of a mouse on four feet, 10" long. Marked "WHW / Made in Austria / Hagenauer Wien." *Courtesy of Christie's, New York.*

Center: A sheet-metal figure in the form of a dachshund with his nose to the ground, 16.5" long. Marked "WHW / Hagenauer Wien." This is a classic example of Hagenauer's skill in working with sheet metal. *Courtesy of Christie's, New York.*

Right: A stylized metal dish in the form of a dove standing on a circular base, 7.5" tall. Marked "WHW / Made in Austria." Another example of Hagenauer's work in repoussé from before World War II. *Courtesy of Christie's, New York.*

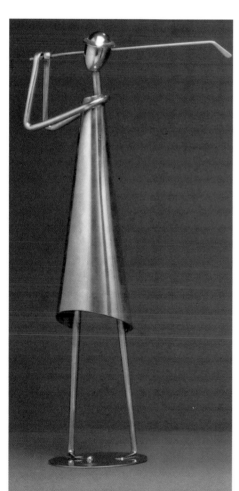

Left:
A polished brass figure of a female golfer, 15" tall. Marked "WHW / Hagenauer Wien / Made in Austria / Franz." *Courtesy of Christie's, New York.*

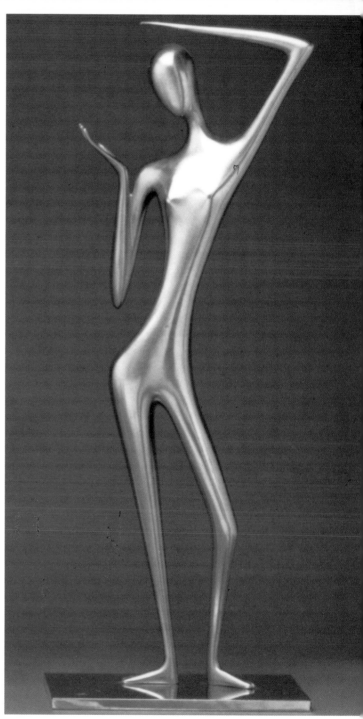

A chrome-plated cast bronze in the form of a slender nude, 16.5" tall. Marked "WHW / Hagenauer Wien / Franz." *Courtesy of Christie's, New York.*

A fine and rare hand-hammered brass sculpture, 29" tall. This sculpture rests on a flattened rectangular base, supporting a curved branch with a profusion of finely hammered, stylized leaves. Marked "WHW / Made in Austria / Hagenauer Wien." *Courtesy of Christie's, New York.*

A pair of chrome-plated sheet-metal masks in the form of a young man and woman with angular features, each 13.5" tall. Marked "WHW / Hagenauer Wien / Franz / 1023." *Courtesy of Christie's, New York.*

A trio of life-sized musicians in chrome-plated sheet metal. The group includes a stylized saxophone player, piano player, and drummer, each composed of numerous pieces of flexible sheet metal. Marked "WHW / Hagenauer Wien / Made in Austria." These jazz players were offered in several sizes, starting at less than 20" tall. These items are avidly sought by collectors, as is indicated by their current values. *Courtesy of Christie's, New York.*

Bottom center: A cast and plated figural mirror formed as stylized monkey, 17" tall. Marked "WHW / Hagenauer Wien."

Center right: A 10"-tall bronze figural group on a polished oval base, depicting a stylized nude figure of a woman with two leashed hounds. Marked "WHW / Made in Austria / Hagenauer Wien."

Center: A figural metal clock in the form of a kneeling female nude, 15" tall. Marked "Hagenauer Wien / Made in Austria" with touchmark.

Bottom left and right: Five metal cordials with female nudes as bases, 5.5" tall. Marked with Hagenauer touchmark and "Made in Austria."

Left center: A 20"-long cast bronze figure of a greyhound leaping forward. Marked "WHW / Made in Austria / 1166 / Franz."

Top left and right: A pair of 18.25"-tall metal candlesticks, each formed of four cylindrical standards intersected by a sphere with removable bobeches. Marked "WHW / Made in Austria" and engraved "20 C-FOX."

Top center: Flat-sided 'boxer' figures, 23.5" long by 16" tall. Marked with Hagenauer touchmark and "Franz / Hagenauer Wien / Made in Austria / 1087/88." *Courtesy of Christie's, New York.*

A pair of metal busts, one formed as a bust of a woman with an elongated face and wearing one earring. The other formed as her male companion wearing a bow tie. 19.25" tall. "WHW / Franz / Hagenauer Wien / Made in Austria. *Courtesy of Christie's, New York.*

A mischievous black and bronze devil, 6" tall. His wings and the baseball bat behind his back are made of polished, brass-colored bronze. Missing its base. *Courtesy of Richard Bell.*

A brown-patinated cast bronze figure depicting Jesus in prayer, 9" tall. Marked "Hagenauer Wien / Made in Austria / Handmade." Hagenauer made several styles of religious figures. *Author's collection.*

A black-patinated cast bronze figure of Jesus with his arms extended, 6" tall. Marked "WHW /
Made in Austria / Hagenauer
Wien / Handmade." This is one of
the easier items to reproduce because of its simple shape and lack
of intricate detail **(see the photograph on page 132)**. *Courtesy of
Rogers Ellingsworth.*

A green-patinated cast bronze
Madonna, 4.5" tall. Marked
"Hagenauer Wien / Made in Austria / Handmade." Mary's halo
was made from a small rolled bar
and is inserted in a drilled hole in
her head. *Author's collection.*

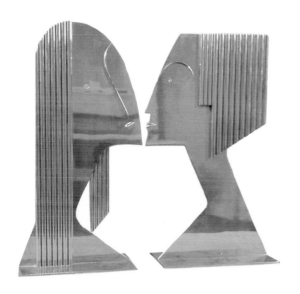

A pair of polished brass and chrome-plated figures in the form of stylized busts, 24" tall. Marked "WHW / Made in Austria / Franz / Hagenauer Wien." *Courtesy of Dawson's Auction Co.*

A 24"-tall mirror with a stylized sheet-metal figure of a curly-headed woman atop. This rests on a cast bronze pedestal supported by a typical Hagenauer sheet-metal base. Marked "WHW / Made in Austria / Hagenauer Wien / Handmade." *Courtesy of Infante and Lasorda.*

An 8" pair of formed sheet-metal bookends in the form of rearing cats. Marked "Made in Austria." *Courtesy of Marjorie Levitt.*

A black and polished brass stamped sheet-metal ashtray, 3.75" x 4.75". Marked "Karl / WHW / Made in Austria / Hagenauer Wien." *Author's Collection.*

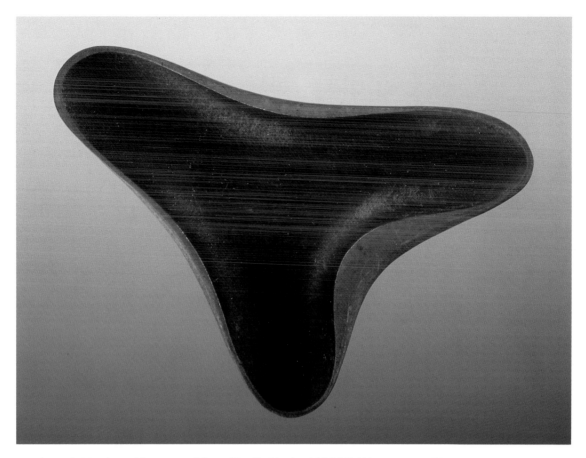

A cast, black and bronze ashtray, 5" x 3". Marked "WHW / Hagenauer Wien / Made in Austria." *Author's collection.*

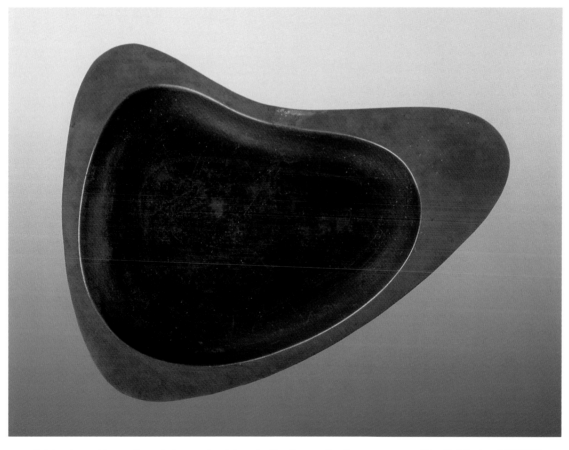

A black and brass hand-shaped ashtray in the form of a boomerang, 6" x 4". Marked "WHW / Hagenauer Wien / Made in Austria / Handmade." *Author's collection.*

A cast black and bronze ashtray in the form of a stylized fish, 5" long. Marked "WHW / Made in Vienna Austria / Hagenauer Wien." *Author's collection.*

A cast, black and bronze ashtray, 4" x 4". Marked "WHW / Hagenauer Wien / Made in Vienna Austria." *Author's collection.*

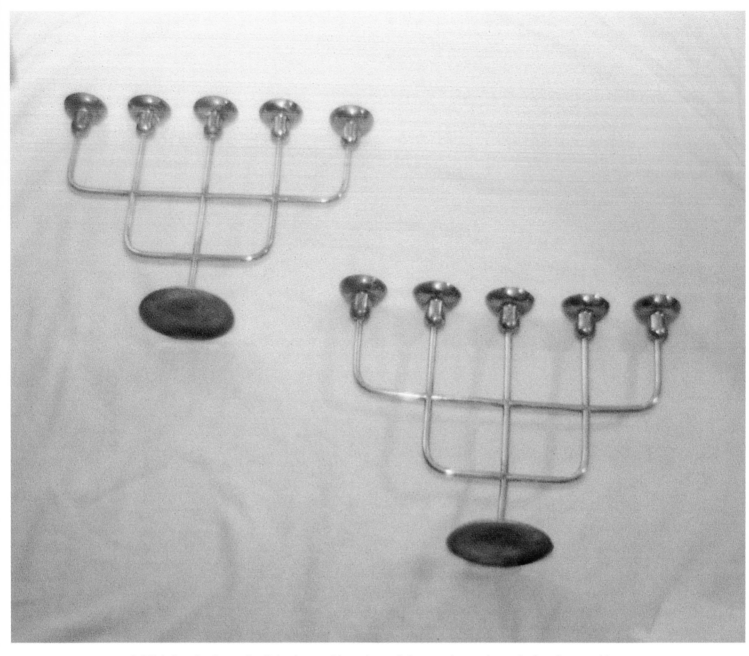

A 20"-tall pair of candlesticks, formed from brass tubes and spun brass bobeches and base. Marked "WHW / Made in Austria." *Courtesy of Michael Westman.*

Rena Rosenthal's association with Hagenauer and Vienna in general is confusing because of a lack of documented information; currently, there are more questions than answers. However, there are some pieces of information that seem accurate.

Rena Rosenthal was a retailer who operated a specialty shop in New York City's fashionable Waldorf Astoria Building during the 1940s and 1950s. She advertised in trade journals and magazines. In her shop she carried Hagenauer merchandise, amongst other things. She also had items designed and made for her exclusively, some of them by Hagenauer—indicated by the presence of both Hagenauer and Rena Rosenthal touchmarks. (Hagenauer did the same thing for other department stores, including Gimbels and Wanamakers.) I believe that other Austrian factories made items for Rosenthal as well, including Baller and Bosse, which I believe is evident in the Rosenthal merchandise shown in this book.

This 5.875"-tall cast figure is a black and bronze cherub with a bow on a 2.75"-diameter base. This piece is unusual in that it is marked "WHW / Hagenauer Wien / Made in Austria" as well as "Rena." *Courtesy of Ed and Helen Tobin.*

A chrome-plated bronze and carved wood figure in the form of a peasant woman, 7.5" tall. Marked "WHW / Atelier Hagenauer Wien / Made in Austria." This piece is also marked "Rena." *Courtesy of Ed and Helen Tobin.*

There are also some pieces marked with an RR touchmark only; these are of a quality represented in Hagenauer's work *(see page 70 top)* and of a style similar to Hagenauer's.

Lastly, there are some "RR"-marked pieces of a quality lower than that of Hagenauer's work *(see page 70 bottom)* and of a style unlike Hagenauer's. The explanation for these is a matter of speculation; did Hagenauer sell factory 'seconds' to Rena Rosenthal? Did they design a less costly line of items for her? Did she design some of the items herself for Hagenauer to produce? Did other factories manufacture for her? I believe all these questions can probably be answered yes.

These differences and doubts are all reflected in the value of the Rena Rosenthal merchandise available on the market. An item marked "RR" in the same style and size as one marked "WHW" will not command as high a price. Very little interest exists for poor-quality RR merchandise, but Hagenauer-style merchandise marked "RR" should be valued based on its own merit.

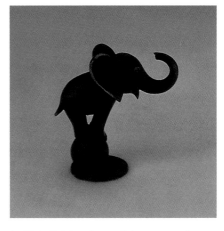

A 4"-tall black and bronze elephant standing on a ball. Marked with the Rena Rosenthal touchmark, "Made in Austria." *Courtesy of Enticements.*

A 3"-long polished cast bronze figure in the form of a lion. Marked with the Rena Rosenthal touchmark, and "Made in Austria." The high quality of this bronze casting is typical of Hagenauer's workmanship. *Author's collection.*

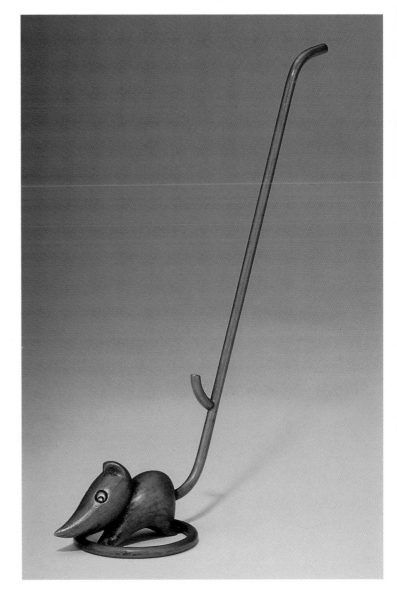

A polished cast bronze ring holder in the form of a mouse, 12" tall. Marked with the Rena Rosenthal touchmark, "Made in Austria." *Author's collection.*

A black-patinated cast bronze figure of a hunter and hound, 3" long x 2" high. Marked with the Rena Rosenthal touchmark, "Made in Austria." *Author's collection.*

A black and bronze casting of an Asian peasant carrying plastic salt and pepper shakers, 6" tall. Marked with the Rena Rosenthal touchmark, "Made in Austria." This Rena Rosenthal piece was not made by Hagenauer, apparent from the poor quality of its design and finish. *Courtesy of Lee Hargrave.*

A black-patinated cast figure of a mother and baby, 3.75", combined with a 2.5" child in black-patinated cast bronze. Each marked with the Rena Rosenthal touchmark, "Made in Austria." *Courtesy of Bruce Horton.*

A cast, black and bronze warrior with a brass shield, 9" tall. Marked with the Rena Rosenthal touchmark, "Made in Austria." This piece is missing its brass spear. *Courtesy of David James.*

A black-patinated cast bronze warrior with brass shield and spear, 8" tall. Marked with the Rena Rosenthal touchmark, "Made in Austria." *Courtesy of Sandra Moran.*

A stylized trio of cast, black and bronze warriors. Marked with the Rena Rosenthal touchmark, "Made in Austria." Please note the unusual headdress and grass skirts. *Private collection.*

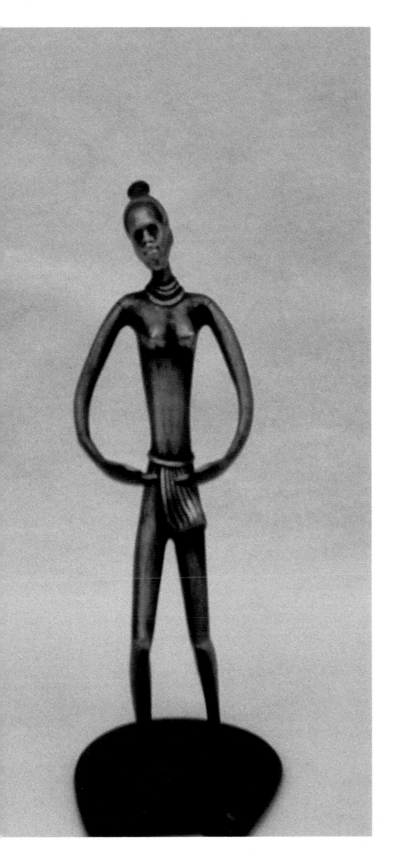

A brown-patinated bronze figure of a Nubian, missing its bowl, 8" tall. Marked with the Rena Rosenthal touchmark, "Made in Austria." *Private collection.*

A cast, black-patinated warrior with a brass spear and shield, 3.75" tall. Marked with the Rena Rosenthal touchmark, "Made in Austria." *Courtesy of Enticements.*

A 2.5"-tall pair of brown-patinated, cast Bavarians. Unmarked. *Courtesy of Richard Faber.*

Hagenauer: In Conclusion

The firm of Hagenauer has influenced metalware production for nearly a century, and their products span the spectrum of metalware manufacturing. Their influence on twentieth-century design will continue to be important in the future because of the interest of collectors of these easily recognized styles–ranging from castings less than 2 inches tall to master pieces in plated sheet metal standing 2 feet tall, commanding several thousand dollars on today's market. The manufacturing processes they represent exhibit only the finest of quality in materials and design.

Their subject matter and expression seem endless, from comic relief to deep pondered thought; they exist for whimsy and fun, for everyday use, for you and me. They were not made for museums, although that is where they belong. They were made our homes and offices. They are valuable, collectible, available, and often affordable, and, as the demand for them increases, they will disappear from the marketplace. The time for them has come, as it should, and I, for one, am happy to have made their acquaintance.

Baller and Bosse

BALLER
AUSTRIA

BOSSE
AUSTRIA

Baller and Bosse are two other Austrian factories whose Hagenauer-style items are often found on the market. Merchandise made by both of these firms is often mistaken for Hagenauer even though they are clearly marked. The styles are similar, probably because of Hagenauer's influence on the market. Much to their credit, no attempts to copy seem apparent. Like Hagenauer, their styles are unique, each manufacturer developing its own designs. Their standards for quality of manufacture and finish were not quite as high as Hagenauer's, though, and the materials they used were less costly. Most of their production is small cast 'black and bronze' decorative items. (The 'black and bronze' style of merchandise is characterized by a heavy coating of black coloring against a polished bronze surface the color of yellow brass. Most Baller and Bosse items are stylized, and very few furnishings are available. Ash trays **(see the photograph on page 76),** ring holders and candle holders should be considered unusual.

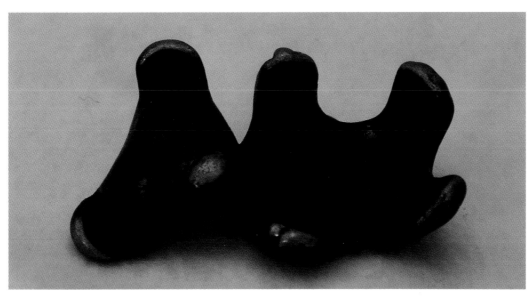

A 2.75" cast figure, black and bronze, in the form of a reclining bear. Probably used as an ashtray. Marked "Baller / Austria." *Courtesy of Jeffrey and Coco.*

A 1.5"-tall cast cat, black and bronze. Marked "Baller / Austria." *Courtesy Marjorie Levitt.*

A cast, black and bronze candleholder in the form of an elephant, 3.5" tall. Marked "Baller / Austria." *Courtesy of Jeffrey and Coco.*

A cast, black and bronze figure in the form of a mouse, 2" long. Not marked. *Author's collection.*

A cast, polished, yellow-colored bronze ashtray in the form of a hand, 5" long x 3" high. Marked "Baller / Austria." *Author's collection.*

Left:
A cast, black and bronze figure in the form of a kneeling woman, 1.875" tall. This abstract figure is marked "Baller / Austria." *Courtesy of Bruce Horton.*

A cast, black and bronze figure in the form of a saxophone player, 2.5" tall. Marked "Bosse / Austria." *Courtesy of Bruce Horton. .*

A pair of cast, black and bronze figures in the form of the zodiac signs for Scorpio and Sagittarius, 2" and 1.75" respectively. Both marked "Bosse / Austria." *Courtesy of Richard Faber.*

A cast, black and bronze figure in the form of a hunter and dog, 2.75" tall. Marked "Bosse / Austria." *Courtesy of Bruce Horton.*

A cast, black and bronze figure in the form of a bull candleholder, 3" long. Marked "Bosse / Austria." *Author's collection.*

A cast bronze ashtray on a marble base in the form of a stylized guitar player, 12" tall. Marked "Made in Austria" (scratched into base). Even though this figure appears to be Hagenauer style, Hagenauer is not known to have created this type on a marble base. *Courtesy of Lon Manning.*

Currently, very little is known about either of these firms. Bosse ceramic items in a Wiener Werkstätte style are often discovered (according to reliable sources), but they don't command the same prices or interest in the antique market. It would appear by examining marks on their metalware pieces that they were made either before 1914 or not for export (which seems unlikely), because they were not marked "Made in." Baller and Bosse items are gaining more favor with collectors as they become better recognized. Prices for their metalwares are lower than for similar Hagenauer pieces, as is their supply. They will become more valuable as time goes on. Like Hagenauer, these items might soon disappear from the market.

A cast bronze figure in the form of a lady playing the cymbals on a marble ashtray base, 3.5" tall. Marked "Made in Austria" (scratched into base). *Courtesy of Marjorie Levitt.*

A cast bronze girl with dog on a marble base, 7.25" tall. Marked "Made in Austria" (scratched into marble base). *Courtesy of It's Your Turn.*

A stamped sheet-metal match holder in the form of an owl, 5" tall. Marked "RASPER / AUSTRIA." *Courtesy of Francesco Johnson.*

A black painted, pierced steel candle holder, 6" tall. Marked "RASPER / AUSTRIA." *Courtesy of Glen Leroux.*

Chapter 3
Germany

ermany has been a highly industrialized country since the industrial revolution. They have always been a world leader in industrial output and it was no different in metalware manufacturing. This chapter will explore the changes in Germany from 1900 through the Bauhaus Era and compare two important collecting fields. Again, the order is based on chronology.

WMF (est. 1856)

In 1856, the metalware manufacturing firm known today as WMF (Wurtembergishe MetalwarenFabrik) was formed in Geislingen, a city in the state of Wurtemberg, Germany. Daniel Straub and his new partners Friedrich and Louis Schweizer began production of metal goods under the name Straub and Schwiezer. At this time, Wurtemberg was already a major metalworking industrial area. Cast iron goods from Wasseralfingen, copper and tin from Esslingen, and brass from Ludswigberg, Stuttgart and Ulm, combined with bronze and metal foundries from Turingen, were all available. Geislingen, because of its location had a distinct advantage in manufacturing. It was an area with a history and supply of skilled craftsmen, whose families had worked in the ivory-carving industry which flourished in the early fifteenth century.

The firm of Straub and Schwiezer employed a labor force of approximate sixty workers in 1856, producing copper and brass household items, plated and patinated to look bronze. They also manufactured "Sheffield Plate" resembling silver. Straub and Schwiezer produced catalogs in 1856, 1859, and 1863.

In 1866, the Schwiezer brothers left the firm and Straub was joined by his son, Heinrich. This new alliance, called Straub und Sohn, produced a catalog in 1876 illustrating 966 different tableware, hollowware, and flatware items. Their trade at this point was primarily in lathe-turned and rolled milled plated goods.

In 1880 Straub and Sohn decided to reshape their manufacturing methods and began electro-plating merchandise. This change brought a dramatic increase in their business. Electro-plating enabled merchandise to be plated in its finished shape rather than by the rolled copper plating process earlier used. This new plating process also allowed for the use of a less costly base metal. Also in 1880, the firm of Straub and Sohn merged with the firm of A. Ritter and Co. of Stuttgart to form the firm of "Wurttembergische MetalwarenFabrik" or, as we know it today, WMF.

By 1881 Daniel Straub had retired as director of the firm and was succeeded by Carl Haegele, formerly of A. Ritter & Co. In 1883, the firm added a glassworks, where they made inserts for their glass-lined metalware items. In 1883, they employed over five hundred workers. In 1889 they purchased the firm of Klumpp & Co, whose specialty was the production of electrotype bronze statues and busts with copper-deposited coating; this patented process proved of much value to the firm. During the last decade of the 1800s, they printed catalogs in three different languages.

By 1900, WMF was a world leader in industrial metalware production with shops and showrooms all over Europe. Their firm produced classic Beidermeir and Rococo styles, popular Jugendstil (Art Noveau) designs and new twentieth-century German designs. In 1900 they employed 3500 workers and operated factories in several German and European cities.

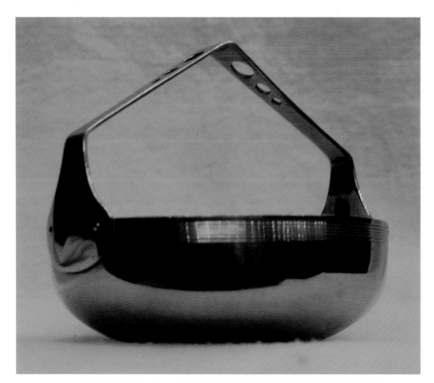

A 4.75" x 4" silver-plated bowl marked "WMF." This piece was made in 1910. *Courtesy of Gloria Dunetz- Montage.*

A segmented glass candy dish in a silver-plated brass holder with handles, 11.75" x 7". Marked with the 'ostrich in a diamond' mark of WMF. Note the use of the square motif. *Courtesy of The Drawing Room of Newport.*

A bronze-colored copper cup with an applied natural cane handle, 3.25" diameter. Marked "WMF / Germany." This highly decorated item has the full beehive mark of 1910 and is a classic example of WMF's twentieth-century manufacture. *Courtesy of Grams and Pennyweights.*

A copper teapot on a black wrought iron stand, 18" tall. Marked "WMF / 14" with the company's 'ostrich in a diamond' logo. *Courtesy of Sal and Deborah Silvestro.*

A nickel-plated samovar, 14" tall. Marked with the WMF 'ostrich in a diamond' logo. *Courtesy of Harriet Rossow.*

A copper handled tray, 18" x 12". Marked "WMF." Note the decoration. *Courtesy of Glen LeRoux.*

A set of six wine goblets and a decanter, 6" tall and 8" tall respectively, made of silver-plated copper. Marked "WMF." *Courtesy of Infante and Lasordo.*

A set consisting of an 18" brass decanter, a tray, and six cup holders. Marked with the 'ostrich in a diamond' logo typical of WMF. *Courtesy of Harriet Rossow.*

A bronze-colored reticulated vase made of copper, 3.5" tall x 2.75" diameter. Marked "WMF" with a tower in a circle. *Courtesy of Evelyn Gordon.* ,

A reticulated, silver-plated copper candy dish, 11.5" long. Marked "WMF / Germany." *Courtesy of Savage Mills.*

A reticulated, silver-plated copper vase, 7.25" tall. Marked "WMF / Germany." *Courtesy of Savage Mills.*

A silver-plated copper flower dish,
6" diameter x 5" tall. Marked "WMF
/ Germany." *Author's collection.*

A silver-plated porcelain creamer,
3.75" diameter. Marked "WMF."
Author's collection.

Most of WMF's merchandise was designed in their own shops, inspired by demand for the style of the day. By 1914, WMF was the largest metalware manufacturer in Europe, with a work force of 6000 laborers producing thousands of items for a worldwide market. They had showrooms in Paris, Berlin, Munich, Frankfurt, and London. Their products were known around the world. They exhibited in shows all over Europe and won several awards for their designs and manufacture.

The manufacturing techniques used by WMF were state-of-the-art throughout their existence, of the highest quality. Their product line consisted of all the most popular styles. Based on their production, large quantities of catalogs and merchandise from this firm ought to be readily available on today's antique market; however, they are not. Items by WMF are highly sought by both European and American collectors in all their popular styles. Merchandise was manufactured with such durable materials and high style that much of it is still in use today by the original purchasers and their families. What little merchandise that does make it to the American secondary market seems reasonably priced, though it is often not recognized as WMF. Their German twentieth-century style (Art Deco) metalware is almost impossible to find; it is of high interest to the collector and commands high values.

Deutcher Werkbund (1907–1930)

The Deutcher Werkbund, founded by German-born Herman Muthesius (*1867-1927*) in 1907, was an association of artists, designers, and industrialists. It was formed to give craftsmen due credit. The concept of Total Art was stressed, as it was in Vienna. The Deutcher Werbund's theories became international, spreading to Austria in 1910, to Switzerland in 1913, and to Sweden and England in 1915. By 1930 it had reached its peak, uniting artists from all over Europe. Their exhibition of decorative art arose from the need to create something new, to distinguish their period with an art which was original and spoke to the masses, combining art and industry. In spite of the Werkbund's popularity its concepts were not universally accepted. Many firms, including WMF, were not associated.

A 2.5"-tall pair of silver-plated cup holders marked "B" (in a circle), "OX" (in a circle), "345." *Courtesy of Gloria Dunetz-Montage.*

𝒯𝒽ℯ 𝐵𝒶𝓊𝒽𝒶𝓊𝓈 (1919-1933)

Out of the Deutcher Werkbund grew the Bauhaus, an idea formulated by Walter Gropius. In 1919, architects, sculptors, painters, and craftsman formed an association of a new kind, free of barrier-forming class distinctions. The Bauhaus was a union between the Arts and Crafts School and the Weimar Academy. Teaching was based upon the study of form and color and on practical craftsmanship. Its principal achievement was providing opportunities for students to create items for use in industry.

A cast bronze ash receptacle, 4.375" long. Marked "Aubök / Made in Austria." This figure, though marked "Austria," was actually done by Karl Aubök, a student of Joseph Itten at Bauhaus in Weimer, Germany. *Courtesy of David Roth.*

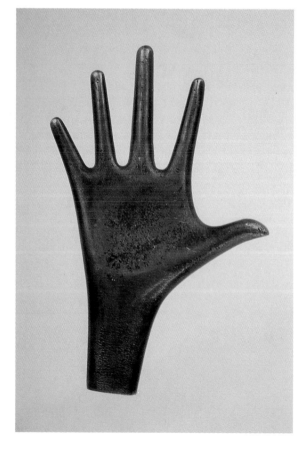

Karl Aubök's stamped mark.

A brown-patinated, cast bronze figure in the form of a right hand, 3.5" long. Marked "Aubök / Made in Austria." *Author's collection.*

A polished, cast bronze ashtray, 6.25" long. Marked "Aubök / Made in Austria." *Courtesy of David Roth.*

The Bauhaus metalshop was developed by Christien Dell in Weimar, Germany, in 1922. (Dell's predecessor, a master craftsman named Kopka, had proved unsuitable: his early artistic leadership was unsteady, and his artistic criteria were revised too often.) Johannes Itten was supervisor of the metalshop until 1923. He was succeeded by Laszlo Moholy-Nagy, who remained as supervisor at Weimar until 1925, when he moved to Dessau. After Moholy-Nagy's departure in 1928 the metalshop was no longer run independently, but was consolidated with other shops concerned primarily with the production of lighting fixtures.

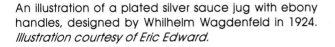

An illustration of an ashtray executed in bronze, designed by Marianne Brandt in 1924. *Illustration courtesy of Eric Edward.*

An illustration of a plated silver sauce jug with ebony handles, designed by Whilhelm Wagdenfeld in 1924. *Illustration courtesy of Eric Edward.*

An illustration of a bronze teapot with ebony handles, designed by Marianne Brandt in 1924. *Illustration courtesy of Eric Edward.*

An illustration of a coffeepot designed by Whilhelm Wagdenfeld in 1924. *Illustration courtesy of Eric Edward.*

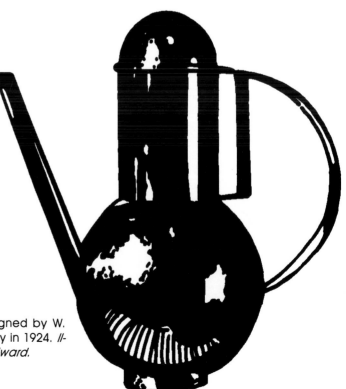

An illustration of a jug designed by W. Rössiger and Freidrich Marby in 1924. *Illustration courtesy of Eric Edward.*

94

Artists and craftsmen of the Bauhaus (including Marianne Brandt, Wilhelm Wagdenfeld, Otto Rittweger, K.J. Jucker, Wolfgang Rössiger, Josef Knau, Josef Albers and Wolfgang Tümpel) did exceptional work. Everyday furnishings were produced in brass (plated and polished), iron, German silver, and silverplate, combined with exotic woods and glass. Forms were often complicated and had a sculptured affect. Styles and techniques were similar to those of the Wiener Werkstätte and were derived from students and craftsmen.

The Bauhaus was closed by the Nazis in 1933. After a four-year hiatus, they reopened in the United States. This "New Bauhaus" later became the Chicago Institute of Design.

Bauhaus products are easily recognized because of the similarity in their style and design; however, items produced by the approximately 1200 artists and students trained at the Bauhaus (like those of other top European artists from this period) are difficult to find. Judging from the volumes of literature on the subject, interest in Bauhaus designs is very high; there are many collectors in this important field. The few Bauhaus items shown in this reference are representative of those available on the antique market today.

A polished brass bowl, 6.25" diameter. Marked "KWHAXORLE, Munchen." *Courtesy of David Roth.*

A handled, covered humidor, 11" tall x 4.5" diameter. This bronze-colored polished copper piece is marked "H.P.Groth." *Courtesy of David Roth.*

A bronze-colored copper bowl, 9.25" x 4.25", on a 1"-tall repoussé base. Marked "Eichener," with a crown in a square with a line above, and the numeral 2. *Courtesy of Jack Papadinis.*

A 5"-tall copper tumbler. Marked "G. Baader Bayrischzell." *Courtesy of Glen LeRoux.*

A nickel-plated bronze match holder, 5" tall. Marked "E. Hartmann / Metalwaren / Munchen." *Courtesy of Gloria Dunetz-Montage.*

The mark on the E. Hartmann match holder. *Courtesy of Gloria Dunetz-Montage.*

A set consisting of a tinned copper creamer, 3" diameter, and a covered sugar bowl, 4.5 " diameter. Marked "HANDERBEIT," probably German. *Courtesy Michael Westman Antiques.*

A four-piece polished copper coffee set on a tray. Marked "GBN" in a diamond. The coffee pot stands 11" high. *Author's collection.*

A copper-handled oil lamp, 6" tall. *Courtesy of Dennis Hancin.*

A chrome-plated bronze candlestand, 11" tall. Marked "GAENMSB," probably German. *Courtesy of Dennis Hancin.*

A black-painted sheet-metal figure in the form of a stylized violinist, 9.25" tall. Marked "Made in West Berlin / USA Sector / Germany." This item was manufactured by an unknown maker after World War II. Related pieces–a ballerina, a jazz band, and a penguin–have been found bearing the same marks. *Private collection.*

Ferdinand Preiss (b. 1882)

Ferdinand Preiss was born in 1882 to a family of ivory-carvers. After being orphaned at the age of fifteen, he apprenticed with Philip Willman and later worked as a modeler in Milan. In 1905, he joined the firm of Carl Haebler in Baden-Baden. In 1906, he moved to Berlin and opened a shop with Arthur Kassler, which they called Preiss and Kassler. When they expanded in 1910 and joined with Robert Kionsek of the Berlin Brass Foundry, they shortened the name to PK. They hired ivory-carvers and began to produce chryselphantine (bronze and ivory) sculptures. In 1914, the firm employed about six ivory-carvers.

After closing for World War I, they reopened in 1919 and by 1925 had hired ten sculptors. Preiss designed most of PK's production. They produced sculptures of children, nudes, Amazons, dancers, bathing beauties, Olympians, and sportsmen and -women in bronze and ivory, as well as in sterling silver. Often his subjects were well-known figures like Ada May, Sonia Henie, and Brigitte Helm, to name a few.

Berlin was a center for artists, including Professor Otto Poerzl, Dorothea Charol, Rudolph Kaesbach, and Phillipe, all of whom were commissioned by PK to produce figures for them. Rosenthal und Maeder used the same artists to produce bronze statuary for them also. These items were marked "RUM." PK took over their production in 1929.

Cast bronze and ivory sculpture by Ferdinand Preiss or PK are actively sought by collectors. Merchandise, if original, is and has been commanding high prices at auction. Very few items are offered for sale by antique dealers or at private sales. Because of their high value, they are often reproduced, and items of dubious authenticity are offered on the market. Therefore, you should know your source and your merchandise when purchasing items of this quality. (See Chapter 6 for a further discussion of reproductions.)

A bronze and ivory figure of a stylish lady, 16" tall. Marked "Paris / ROYF / 1930 F / Preiss." *Private collection.*

Chapter 4
France

The French Art Deco metalware market, not unlike the French antique market, is driven by art—as well it should be, since the French themselves are driven by art. France (particularly Paris) has been a center of art since the eighteenth century, and became especially important at the turn of the twentieth century.

Chiparus, Puiforcat & Other French Artists

Many French artists and French manufacturers produced metalware items for sale. Artists like D.H. Chiparus (born Rumanian) and Raymond Subes (born Hungarian) came to Paris to make their way. Firms like Suè et Mare and Christofle produced high-style French Art Deco for the well-to-do French marketplace. Most of these luxury items were highly sought in their day and were purchased by museums and wealthy collectors when they were manufactured. The French market was interested only in the finest quality merchandise, and they would pay the price. This fact is reflected in the high values and limited availability of merchandise offered for sale today.

At the turn of the century, French artists and studios were producing typical French-style Art Noveau furniture, furnishings and metalware, and they were slow to change. While Vienna and Germany were producing Modern Trend merchandise as early as 1898, the French did not get started (and then only in their own way) until many years later. According to most authorities, it was the French who first used the term "Art Deco," in conjunction with the "Le Exposition des Arts Dècoratifs" in Paris in 1925. Before 1906 most French metalware was uninspired, derivative, overly complicated, and unattractive. The Salon d'Autumne's displays of the decorative arts in 1912 allowed artists and metalworkers to inspire each other. This marked the end of the era of the solitary metalworker. A change had been brought on by the introduction of new machinery and new techniques for treating and finishing metal. However, this new machinery created a problem for the French artists: it forced mass production to defray the cost of technology.

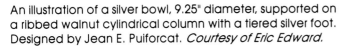
An illustration of a silver bowl, 9.25" diameter, supported on a ribbed walnut cylindrical column with a tiered silver foot. Designed by Jean E. Puiforcat. *Courtesy of Eric Edward.*

An illustration of a 10.25 " diameter silver tureen with lapis lazuli handles. *Courtesy of Eric Edward.*

This change did not suit Jean Puiforcat (1897-1945), a popular French Art Deco metalware artist. He was interested only in producing one-of-a-kind items in expensive materials. He had learned his trade in his father's workshop and had studied sculpture with Louis Aimè Lejuene, and first displayed his wares at the Salon d'Autumne in 1921. In 1922 the Museum of Decorative Arts purchased one of his designs–a coffee pot in silver with lapis-lazuli handles. A most important silversmith, he approached his craft from an esthetic and philosophical point of view. He often contrasted his silver work with gold and other materials, like lapis or exotic woods. Puiforcat was hailed as a great innovator. He was a member of the admissions and prize-awarding juries at the 1925 Paris exhibit where his merchandise was displayed. In 1926 he formed a gallery called "Les Cinq," where he exhibited regularly. In 1930 he founded with others the Union Des Artistes Modernes.

French metalware manufacturers were producing clean, modern lines by 1912. The firms of Suè et Mare, Cardeilac, Faberge, and Christofle were receptive to the simplicity and geometry of Art Deco and commissioned artists to design for them. Suè et Mare produced mirrors, lighting fixtures, fire screens, and builder's hardware, often in styles similar to Dagobert Peche of the Wiener Werkstätte. Christofle manufactured tea and coffee sets, soup tureens, samovars, candle stands, and boxes, often in electro-plate. Hungarian artists (including Raymond Subes, Edouard Schenk, Adalbert Szabo, and Jules and Michel Nics), and Rumanian artists (D.H. Chiparus, Fred Perret, Gilbert Poillerat, Robert Merceris, and Paul Kis) all settled in Paris to display their wares.

Constantin Brancusi (1876–1957)

Well-known sculptor Constantin Brancusi (1876-1957), also from Rumania, settled in Paris in 1904. Brancusi studied at the Bucharest Academy of Fine Art and while in Paris studied sculpture with Mercier. A contemporary of Rodin, Brancusi produced statuary in stone, bronze, marble, wood, and plaster. Often his styles were egg-shaped and cylindrical. He seemed obsessed with bird shapes and phallic shapes. His subjects were basic and simple. He often produced the same style over and over again, with slight adjustments to each finished piece–making most examples of his work one-of-a-kind. The quality that he achieved in the production and finish of his sculpture was near perfect. Brancusi, a pre-Cubist, was a great influence on twentieth-century design.

A stylized marble bust of a woman, 18" tall, attributed to C. Brancusi. This figure is Mlle. Pogany, a popular subject often portrayed by Brancusi. Also produced in polished bronze. *Courtesy of The Auction Room Ltd.*

Edgar Brandt (1880-1960)

Probably the most famous French metalsmith known today is Edgar Brandt. He produced metal grates, doors, furniture, and furnishings in copper, brass, bronze, and iron. Brandt worked in conjunction with Ruhlman, Lalique, and Daum Fréres of Nancy among others. His most famous design, the Serpent Lamp, was made in several sizes with glass shades made by Daum. Brandt had served a long apprenticeship. He studied silver and gold, jewelry, and ironwork. He was awarded a third-class membership to the Society of French Artists in 1905, a second-class membership in 1907, first-class in 1908, and finally a full-class membership. In 1923, he received a medal of honor for his designs and workmanship. He was a member of the jury at the Salon d'Automne and a member of the Society of Artists and Decorators.

An illustration of a wrought iron and marble console, 31" tall, constructed of a foliate-design framework set on a marble base. Designed by Edgar Brandt. *Illustration courtesy of Eric Edward.*

Metalware by Edgar Brandt and other top French artists and manufacturers (like the works of top European artists in general) are almost never offered for private sale by dealers. Merchandise is usually offered for sale only at the most renowned auction houses, where it commands high prices.

Articles by lesser-known firms and artists are frequently offered, and can often be purchased at a reasonable price. However, these items require more research to identify, and are often more difficult to price.

Bronze statuary

Bronze statuary in a style similar to that on the French market has been produced by popular artists and firms from other countries and, for comparative purposes, will be included here.

A 15" bronze and ivory figure of a dancer. Marked "CLJR / Colinet / 200." *Courtesy of Richard Wright Antiques.*

A 19" bronze and ivory figure of a girl holding roses. Marked "JD / 82 / LAURRAR." *Courtesy of Richard Wright Antiques. .*

A 20" mate to the previous piece. *Courtesy of Richard Wright Antiques.*

A silver-plated cast bronze figure representing Le'Poirot, 12.5" tall. By Pierre Le'Faquays. Marked "La'Stelle" and "Pierre Le Faquays." *Courtesy of J. B. Antiques.*

A French cold-painted bronze, 21". Unmarked. *Courtesy of Jeff's Vintage.*

A 22"-tall bronze and ivory ballerina on a rouge marble base. Marked "DH Chiparus." *Courtesy of Barry S. Slossberg Inc., Auctioneers.*

(Left) A standing ballerina in silver, ivory and enameled bronze, Art Deco, 24" tall. Marked "Prof. O. Poertzl." *Courtesy of Barry S. Slossberg Inc., Auctioneers.* (Right) A 17"-tall bronze and ivory dancer in a hoop skirt. Marked "Phillipe." *Courtesy of Barry S. Slossberg Inc., Auctioneers*

A 16"-tall bronze lady smoking a cigarette. Marked "Bruno Zach." *Courtesy of Richard Wright Antiques.*

A 12.75"-tall bronze huntress. Marked "Argentor / Vienna." *Courtesy of Richard Wright Antiques.*

A silver-plated bronze and ivory dancing girl on a green marble base, 10.75" tall. Marked "Lorenzl." *Courtesy of Sandra Chadwick.*

A chrome-plated brass bud vase, 9.5" tall. Marked "Made in France." This vase consists of two square-shaped hollow tubes attached to a 4" x 4" chrome-plated base. *Author's collection.*

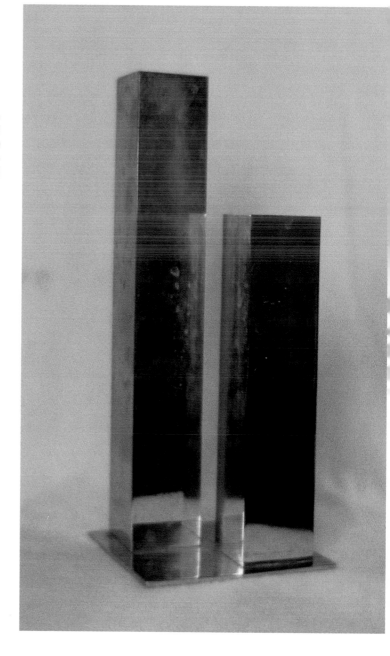

A silver-plated, cast bronze figure of a small deer on a black marble base, 6" tall. Marked "France / Bronze / Rishmann." *Courtesy of Thomas Matarese.*

Throughout the 1920s and 1930s, the Austrian firm of Goldscheider (which closed in 1930) produced items in bronze and in ceramic for the French Art Deco market. Austrian-born designer Joseph Lorenzl and Hungarian-born artist Alexander Kelety produced for this market, as did Frenchmen Pierre Le Faquays. They exhibited in Paris in 1900 and again in 1925 in their own pavilion.

The Paris firm of Etling distributed works by the artist and sculptor Demitre Chiparus, a Rumanian who had settled in Paris. His spectacular chryselphantine figures were often inspired by the theatre and ballet. Other Etling artists include Claire Jeanne Roberte Colinet, born in Brussels, and Austrian Bruno Zach, who often did erotic sculpture. Works by all these artists are commanding high prices on today's antique market.

Chapter 5
Denmark

The Danish metalware market consisted primarily of one early metalware manufacturer of note, the George Jensen Silversmithy. This firm was associated through the years with several Danish silver artists to create some of the most modern and easily recognized Art Deco styles we know today. The firm's influence on modern design continues: many of the more popular styles from the 1940s and 1950s are still being produced today.

Georg Jensen (1866-1935)

Georg Jensen was born in Raadvad, Denmark in 1866. He started his career as a general hand in a foundry and later served an apprenticeship as a brazier. At his parents' urging, Jensen eventually apprenticed as a goldsmith. As a journeyman goldsmith he was schooled in engraving and modeling. Determined to become a sculptor, he modeled a bust of his father as a project for Professor Theabold Stein and was admitted to the Danish Academy of Fine Art, from which he graduated in 1892. During school he earned a living as a goldsmith, and for a short time worked as a modeler producing ceramic items for Bing and Grondöhl. Jensen's own work with gold became successful, however, and in 1899 the Danish Museum of Decorative Art purchased a vase from him entitled "Girl With Jar."

In 1900, Jensen was awarded a major travel grant at the academy and went to Paris to expand his studies. After his return from Paris, Jensen resumed his work for Bing and Grondöhl as a modeler. This proved unsuccessful, so he finally returned to his old craft of goldsmithing to feed his growing family. He was forty years old when he became an independent silversmith and opened his first workshop in 1904. There Jensen created jewelry items and silverwork in a new style unlike anything made in the past. His jewelry was inexpensive and was worked with amber, malachite, moonstones, and opals. His merchandise was made for the middle-class customer. In 1908, Jensen began to make tableware, flatware, and furnishings, and in 1909 a Berlin colleague opened a shop representing Jensen.

A set consisting of a 4.5"-long fork and spoon in sterling silver. Marked "Georg Jensen."
Courtesy of Michael Westman Antiques.

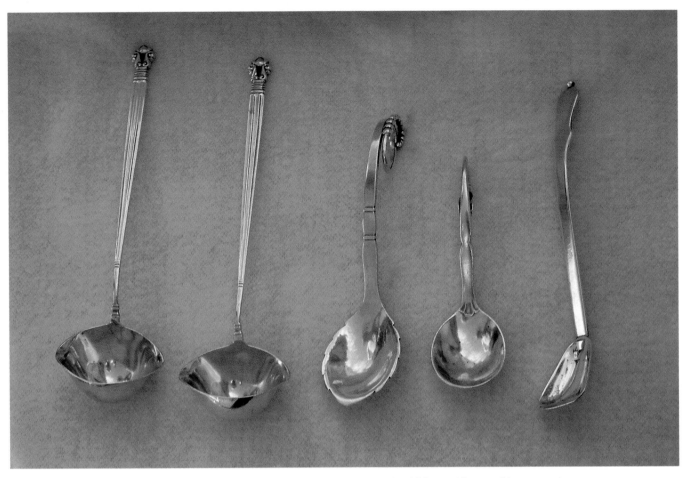

An assortment of sterling silver spoons. Most are marked "Georg Jensen" in an oval.
Courtesy of Green Door Antiques.

A pair of 3"-long sterling silver sugar spoons. Marked "Georg Jensen." *Courtesy of Green Door Antiques.*

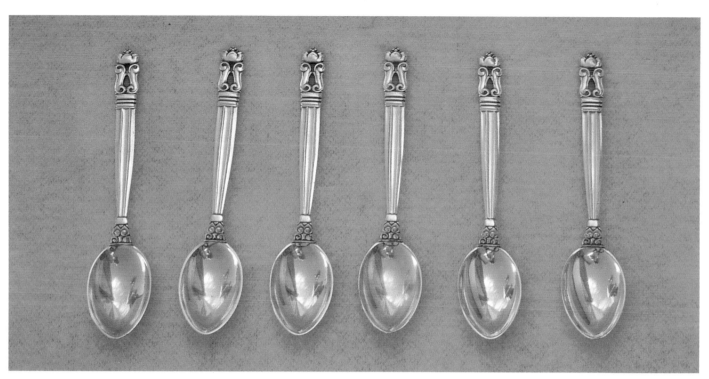

A set of six demitasse spoons, each 5" long. Marked "Georg Jensen." *Courtesy of Green Door Antiques.*

A 7.5"-long sterling silver and lapis bracelet. The interlocking links are small lost wax castings, typical of jewelry manufacture. Marked "JG" in a square. *Courtesy of Soren Jensen.*

A set consisting of an 8" bracelet and a 15" necklace, made from cast links and set with green stones. Marked with a Jensen dot mark that was used from 1915 to 1927. *Courtesy of Soren Jensen.*

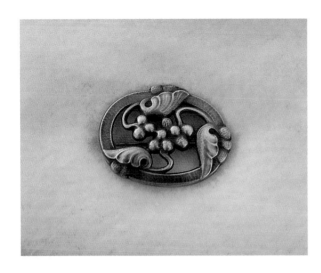

A cast silver pin in the form of an entwined grape vine, 2.5" x 1.5". Marked "Georg Jensen." *Courtesy of Howard Byer.*

A 1.5"-long sterling silver pin. Marked "Georg Jensen." *Courtesy of Jeffrey and Coco.*

A tea set consisting of a 15" tray, a 7" tea pot, and a 3" sugar and creamer. Marked "Georg Jensen." *Courtesy of Soren Jensen.*

A 7"-tall sterling silver water pitcher with an applied black handle. Marked "Georg Jensen in Wendelais / 385 A." *Courtesy of Green Door Antiques.*

A dresser set executed by Georg Jensen, consisting of all the popular accessories. The comb is approximately 12" long. All pieces are marked with a dotted crown. *Courtesy of Soren Jensen.*

A 24" tray from the Georg Jensen dresser set. *Courtesy of Soren Jensen.*

A 10"-diameter plate, marked with an acorn. *Courtesy of Green Door Antiques.*

A fluted Georg Jensen bowl, 5.5" tall x 6" diameter.
The design was made by Johann Rhode in 1917;
this example is a later recast produced in the 1940s.
Courtesy of Jeff's Vintage.

Over the years, the firm of Georg Jensen associated with many
silver designers and artists (including Johan Rohde and Harold Nielsen)
and executed designs by them. After his passing in 1935, his sons
Jorgen Jensen and Sóren Georg Jensen continued to operate the
firm as an important part of twentieth century design. Merchandise
by Georg Jensen Silversmithy is of the highest quality in both style
and manufacture, and is widely sought by collectors today. The
company's products are available and often affordable.

Chapter 6
Reproductions

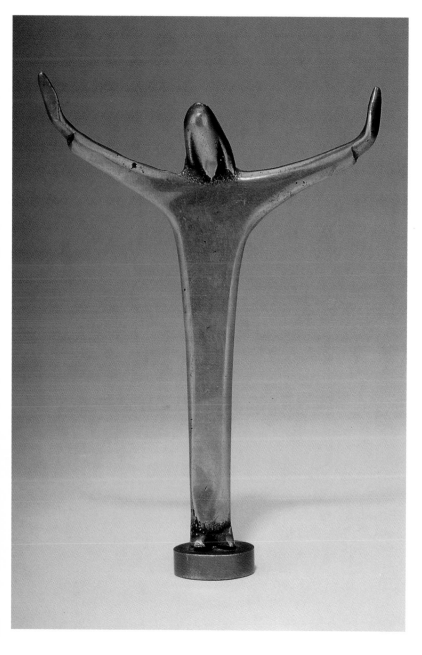

H igh-quality decorative metalware articles (not including holloware, tableware, furnishings, and everyday utilitarian items) manufactured by most of the prominent European Art Deco firms are now being reproduced. Most of the more important artists are represented, including Hagenauer.

A cast, yellow-colored bronze figure of Jesus with arms extended, 6" tall. This is a reproduction, probably cast from the original Hagenauer piece illustrated p. 61. Note the poor quality of finish where the piece is joined to the base, and in the difficult-to-reach areas at the underarms and neck. Unmarked. *Private collection.*

In general, though, making Hagenauer reproductions is not feasible at this time, since the original Hagenauer merchandise is available at prices below the cost of reproducing them. This is not true with better known bronze statuary like those by Chiparus, for example. Chiparus reproductions and reproductions of all of the cabinet-sized chryselphantine types are available for about three to five hundred dollars. Originals of these items are valued at several thousand dollars at top level auctions–unaffordable within most budgets. Reproductions offer opportunities otherwise unavailable to many customers, and I believe they have a place on the market. Of course, any attempt to defraud a customer by selling a reproduction as an original is an abominable act; nobody should ever profit from it.

The 1995 cost to manufacture lost wax cast brass or bronze statuary in small quantities is approximately three hundred dollars. The technology has been around for at least a thousand years; there are foundries, small workshops, and artists using the technique all over the world. They produce for themselves and for industry, casting small pieces for jewelry or huge items for industry. There are specialty founders that cast nothing but decorative items for artists and sculptors, or nothing but building hardware.

A black-patinated and brass figure cast in the form of a stylized cat, 2.5" long. This piece, manufactured in a style resembling Hagenauer's, could not be considered a reproduction, because it does not fulfill the criteria for original Hagenauer designs. Specifically, the cat's legs are molded together, and the cat was cast in one piece rather than being attached to the base as was Hagenauer's custom. Unmarked. *Author's collection.*

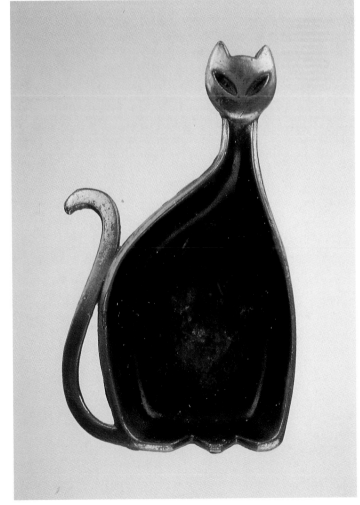

Right:
A 4.5"-long cast spelter cat ashtray in a black and brass style like Hagenauer's. *Author's collection.*

A green-patinated bronze recast, probably from an original Lorenzl, 13" tall. Merchandise of this quality is available at a reasonable price. *Private collection.*

A cast bronze figure probably recast from a D.H. Chiparus bronze, on a simple round marble base, 12" tall. This figure is offered in a cold-painted variety also. *Private collection.*

A cold-painted spelter figure of a girl with a hoop, 13" tall. This figure is a popular recast. *Private collection.*

In addition, there are companies that specialize in reproduction casting for the decorator trades. Foundering brass and bronze is a big business. There are a lot of talented craftsmen who have the technical skill to reproduce top quality merchandise, and a lot of them do. Often reproductions are cast from original molds for entirely legitimate purposes. For example, museums offer reproductions of important works for sale in limited editions, as it is their legitimate right to do. Often (too often) these items are resold as original works by the artist or firms they represent. However, reproductions are fairly easy for knowledgeable customers to recognize because of some noticeable differences from the originals.

First, almost all original artwork or high-quality metalware of any age is marked by the artist or manufacturer. Most of these marks are stamped into the item. Stamps are very costly to produce, requiring a different metalware industry. Most reproduced merchandise is not stamped, which should warn the buyer to be cautious.

Second, today (like yesterday and tomorrow) labor equals money or value, and this can be measured in the quality of style and finish of the merchandise. High-quality merchandise manufactured by top manufacturers is extremely difficult to reproduce. The original manufacturer had specialized expertise and specialized machinery available to him, an interest in the merchandise he was making, and a stake in the future of an item. This concern shows in the finished product. Reproduction cast metalware items, on the other hand, are generally lacking in quality. Specifically, look for pits in the castings from poor quality metal mixing, toolmarks, or file and grinder marks where there should be none. Dark, unfinished areas in places that are hard to reach (like armpits or crevices), uneven patination, coloring, or plating, and screws or fasteners that detract from the item are also indications of reproduced merchandise. Experienced collectors generally look for reasons not to buy an item; the general rule should be "If you have a reason not to buy, don't." If there is any question in your mind about the quality of an item, use it as an excuse for you to pass it by.

Another tip-off about identifying reproductions is often in the price of the article. Items of a questionable price deserve questions! Top-quality merchandise commands top value, and there is a market for it. If an item is valued at $10,000 why should a knowledgeable dealer sell it for much less? (Remember, though, that not all dealers are knowledgeable, and affordable merchandise is not always of a questionable nature.)

Another factor when considering reproductions are articles that have been legitimately manufactured in a style reflecting the influence of a certain artist and are not marked by their maker. For example, an unmarked bronze casting of a dancer in a style like that of F. Preiss may sold legitimately as a reproduction; but later, another party may sell it as an original Preiss. This item is then re-offered to the trade as an original, and may be purchased as such without challenge. Unfortunately, this happens too often. The trade and the public should beware.

Chapter 7

On Collecting

Collecting has often been described (particularly by collectors) as a disease, or at best an addiction. As anyone who collects anything will tell you, it gets into your blood and creates a passion for merchandise and information. Often collectors consciously decide what to collect, but just as often collectors are drawn to their field without any conscious thought. One thing, however, is always true: collecting consumes us in a positive way and enriches our lives unlike anything else.

Metalware collecting is rapidly becoming a popular pastime. An appreciation for metalworking skills is on the rise. Art Deco metalware has always been sought by collectors, and popular Arts and Crafts metalware manufactured by prominent American and European firms is starting to disappear from the market. Metalware articles executed by Wiener Werkstätte and particularly Josef Hoffmann now exist primarily in museum collections. Metalware pieces by Wiener Werkstatte, Josef Hoffmann, Dagobert Peche, the French manufacturers Sue et Mare, Jean Puiforcat, and Edgar Brandt, as well a the chryselephantine statuary by Preiss and Chiparus, and original sculpture by artists including C. Brancusi have reached such a high value that they are out of reach for most collectors. Very little of this merchandise is offered for sale at any price. Decorative bronze and bronze and ivory statuary is offered at top auction houses occasionally, reaching high prices.

However, this is not true with most of the other manufacturers illustrated in this book. Items by Georg Jensen, the firm of WMF, and artists from the Bauhaus school are still available and at reasonable prices. Interest in all of these fields is high and merchandise is easily recognizable. Merchandise made by other German manufacturers is available, and there is a lot of information accessible for reference.

Items made by Hagenauer or made by others in Hagenauer style are now becoming more available on the market. Interest in this easily recognized family firm and style is beginning to peak as collectors and dealers start to recognize and appreciate the style and quality of Hagenauer's unique designs. Their sheet-metal sculptures are the only examples of this type of work available today. The small lost wax cast animals made by Hagenauer are a bargain at any price but are available for any budget. Their ethnographic art is a view never before or since presented. Their merchandise in its day was market-driven and is an indication of the original interest in this popular firm.

Though not reproductions, modern Hagenauer-*style* items are presently being made and offered to the market. Caution when making a large purchase should always be the rule, no matter what your collecting interest might be.

Damaged articles and items with missing pieces or without the correct patina should never be considered at a premium price. The nature of the design of some delicate pieces means that stress-caused bending is often apparent on small, delicate cast features. This should be considered serious damage, since it is very difficult to straighten out without proper care. Bronze by its nature becomes brittle when heated and heat should never be applied to repair damage.

Articles made by Hagenauer were made in large enough quantities that another piece of the same or similar style will soon become available. Let damaged pieces remain where they are unless they are priced so low that they are hard to pass up. Each piece should be priced based on its own merits or lack of them taking all things into consideration.

Pieces by such makers as Baller and Bosse, or bearing the Rena Rosenthal mark, all in a Hagenauer style, are fast becoming appreciated in their own right. Still, seemingly recognizable unmarked items should not be considered by a collector who is only partially knowledgeable, except at a low price.

Bibliography

Ammen, C. W. *Lost Wax Investment Casting,* Blue Ridge Summit, Pa.: Tab Books, 1977

Ammen, C. W. *Casting Brass,* Blue Ridge Summit, Pa.: Tab Books, 1985

Antique Collectors Club. *Art Noveau Domestic Metalwork from Wurtembergisches MetalwarenFabrik 1906* Woodbridge, Suffolk: Antique Collectors Club 1988

Arnason, H. H. *The History of Modern Art,* New York: Harry N. Abrams, Inc., 1968

Brunhammer, Yvonne. *Art Deco Style,* New York: St. Martin's Press, 1984

Curtis, Tony. *The Lyle Antiques and Their Values,* New York: Voor Hoede Publicaties B. V., 1982

Duncan, Alastair *Art Deco* London :Thames and Hudson, 1988

Fusco, Tony *Official identification and price guide to Art Deco* New York : House of Collectibles 1988

Howarth, Thomas. *Charles Rennie Macintosh and the Modern Movement,* New York: Wittenborn Publications Inc., 1953

Hull, Daniel R. *Castings of Brass and Bronze,* Cleveland, Oh.: American Societies of Metals, 1952

Kallir, Jane. *Viennese Design and the Wiener Werkstatte,* New York: George Braziller, 1986

Naylor, Gillian. *The Bauhaus,* London: Studio Vista Limited, 1968

Noever, Peter. *Josef Hoffmann Designs,* Munich: MAK Austrian Museum of Fine Art, 1992

Renwick Gallery. *Georg Jensen Silversmithy,* Washington, D.C.: Smithsonian Museum, 1980

Varnedoe, Kirk. *Vienna 1900 Art Architecture and Design,* New York: Museum of Modern Art, 1986

Wingler, Hans M. *The Bauhaus,* Cambridge, Ma.: M.I. T. Press, 1964

Value Guide

Values listed in this book indicate the price of a similar item in good to excellent condition as most metalware and sculpture should be, except for some allowance for tarnishing (particularly on polished brass or copper items). However merchandise which has tarnished should be of an even color and show no signs of an attempt to repolish. Black finished pieces whether black patinated or black coated should show no signs of stress from bending. Even though some items are missing pieces in the book the values indicated are for complete merchandise with all their pieces. In most cases the values listed indicate a range in which the item was offered for sale or sold at auction. However this is only a guide and should not be considered as the final determining factor in making a purchase. Niether the author nor the publisher assume any responsibilty for its use or missuse.

Pg.	Pos.	Value
8		350-450
15		800-1100
16		700-900
17	T	700-900
17	B	250-350
18		3000-4000
20		250-350
21	TL	150-200
21	TR	150-200
21	BL	100-150
21	BR	150-200
22	TL	150-200
22	ML	100-150
22	TR	150-200
22	B	150-200
22	BR	150-200
23	TL	150-200
23	TR	150-200
23	BL	100-150

Pg.	Pos.	Value
23	BR	150-200
24	TL	150-200
24	TR	150-200
24	BL	150-200
24	BR	150-200
25	L	100-150
25	TR	150-200
25	B	100-150
26	T	150-200
26	B	300-400
27	T	250-350
27	B	250-350
28	T	250-350
28	B	200-300
29		1300-1600
30	T	400-500
30	B	350-450 ea.
31		375-475
32	T	800-1000

Pg.	Pos.	Value
32	B	400-500
33	T	1200-1600
33	BL	250-350
33	BR	250-350
34	TL	250-350
34	TR	250-350
34	BL	250-350
34	BR	500-600
35	T	350-450
35	B	350-450ea.
36		500-600
37	T	600-700
37	B	400-500
38	T	400-500ea
38	B	250-350
39		500-600
40	T	300-400
40	B	350-450
41	T	300-400

Pg.	Pos.	Value
41	B	900-1100
42	T	400-500
42	B	450-550
43	T	800-1000
43	B	400-500
44		4000-6000
45		1500-2000
46	T	11000-15000
46	B	2000-3000ea.
47		2000-3000
48		2000-3000
49		7000-9000
50		6000-8000
51		4000-6000
52		4000-6000
53		7500-9000
54	TL	1000-1500
54	TC	1000-1500
54	TR	1300-1600
54	BL	2400-3000
54	BR	3500-4000
55		9000-13000
56		1200-1600ea.
57		10000-13000ea.
58	BC	3000-4000
58	CR	1600-2100
58	C	3500-4000
58	BLR	300-400ea.
58	LC	1500-2000
58	TLR	1600-2000ea.
58	TC	3000-5000
59		4000-6000ea.
60	TL	350-400
60	L	500-700
61	R	250-300

Pg.	Pos.	Value	Pg.	Pos.	Value	Pg.	Pos.	Value	Pg.	Pos.	Value
62	T	3000-4000ea.	76	TR	75-100	90	B	25-50	115		4500-5500
62	B	5000-6000	76	CR	50-75	91		50-75ea.	116		800-1000
63	T	250-300	76	B	250-300	92	L	200-300	117		1300-1600
63	B	300-350	77	TL	100-150	92	R	150-200	118	L	400-600
64	T	250-300	77	TR	100-150	93		300-400	118	R	150-200
64	B	200-250	77	C	50-75ea.	95		100-150	120		50-100ea.
65	T	250-300	77	BL	100-150	96		700-1000	121	T	50-100ea.
65	B	200-250	77	BR	50-100	97	T	200-250	121	B	100-150ea.
66		1200-1400	78		350-400	97	B	75-125	122	T	50-100ea.
67		400-450	79	L	350-450	98	T	75-125	122	B	2500-3000
68		700-900	79	R	200-300	98	B	200-250	123	T	2200-2800
69	T	150-200	80	T	100-150	99	T	75-125	124	T	300-350
69	L	150-200	80	B	75-100	99	B	50-100	124	C	300-350
69	BR	150-200	82		50-100	100		75-125	124	B	4000-6000 set
70	T	150-200	83	T	450-550	101		100-150	125		2500-3000
70	B	150-200	83	B	100-150	103		7000-9000	126		3000-4000 set
71	T	200-300	84		400-600	106		SPECIAL	128		with set
71	B	250-300	85		200-300	108		8000-9000	130		1500-2100
72	T	300-350	86	T	200-250	109		2800-3000	131		1400-2000
72	B	300-350ea.	86	B	450-550	110		2800-3000	132		10-15
73	L	200-250	87		150-250	111		6000-7000	133	L	10-20
73	R	200-250	88	T	50-100	112		1000-1200	133	R	10-25
74		100-150ea.	88	B	50-100	113		6000-7000	134		200-400
75		125-150	89		100-150	114	L	4000-5000	135		200-400
76	TL	75-125	90	T	25-50	114	R	800-1000	136		200-400

Index

Italic numerals refer to illustrations and photos

Academic Architecture, 13
Albers, Josef , 95
Animals, *18-31, 44, 54, 58, 63, 69, 70, 75-79, 118, 133*
Argentor, 14
Art Noveau, 82
Arts and Architecture, 13
Art and Design , 13
Art et Decoration, 13
Aubök, Karl, 14, *92, 93*

Baller, 14, 67, 75,78, 139
Bauhaus, 5, 14, 81, 92, 95, 138
Beidermeir, 82
Bernauer Samu,15
Bing & Grondöhl, 119
Bookends, *16, 17, 63*
Bosse, 14, 67, 75, 78, 139
Brancusi, Constantin,106, 138
Brandt, Edgar, 107, 138
Brandt, Marianne, 95
Busts, *46, 50-53, 59, 62*

Candle holder, *11, 47, 58, 66, 76, 77, 80, 99*
Cardeilac, 105
Charol, Dorothea, 102
Cherub, 67
Children, *33,34,71*
Chiparus, D. H., 104, 105, 133, 138
Christofle, 104, 105
Cizek, Franz, 40
Clown, *111*

Das Kunstblatt, 13
Daum Freres, 107
Dell, Christien, 93
Deutsche Kunst und Dekoration, 13
Deutcher Werkbund, 91
Devil, 60
Dresser set, *126-129*

Faberge, 105
Female figures, *42, 43, 49-54, 58, 59, 62, 68, 77, 79, 103, 108-110, 112-117, 134-136*
Furniture, *8,107*

Gropius, Walter, 92

Haebler, Carl, 102
Haegele, Carl, 82
Hagenauer, 5, 14, 67, 69, 74, 75, 78, 132, 133, 138, 139
Hagenauer, Carl, 14, 15, 16, 21, 40
Hagenauer, Franz, 31, 40
Hagenauer, Grete,. 31
Hagenauer, Karl, 21, 31,139
Hanak, Anton, 40
Helm, Briitte, 102
Hennie, Sonia, 102
Hoffman, Josef, 7,9, 10, 11, 14, 16, 31, 138

Ink stand, *11*
Itten,Johannes, 93

Jensen, Georg, 5, 119, 120, 138

Jensen, Jorgen, 131
Jensen, Sören, 131
Jewelry, *123,124*
Jirasek, Julius, 32,
Jucker, K. J., 95
Jugendstil, 82

Kassler, Arthur,102
Kionsek, Robert, 102
Kis, Paul, 105
Klimt, Gustave, 10, 11
Klump & Co., 82
Knau, Josef, 95
Kopka, 93

Lalique, 107
L'art Decoratif, 13
Loos, Adolph, 11
Lorenzl, Josef, 14

Macintosh, Charles Rennie, 7, *8,* 9, 10, 12
MacNair, Herbert, 9
Marby,Freidrich, *94*
Masks,*56*
May, Ada,102
McDonald, Francis, 9
McDonald, Margaret, 9
Merceris, Robert, 105
Mirror, *45, 62*
Modern Trend, 5, 7,9, 31, 105
Moholy-Nagy, Laszlo,. 93
Moser, Koloman, 10, 11, 12
Musical, *42, 57, 77-79, 101*
Muthesius, Herman, 91

Nics, Jules and Michel 105
Nielsen, Harold, 131
Nubian, *32,33,39,43,73*

Olbrich, Joseph, 9, 10

Peche, Dagobert, 105, 138
Perret, Fred, 105
Phillipe, 102
PK, 102

Poerzl, Otto, 102
Poillert, Gilbert, 105
Preiss, Ferdinand, 102, 137
Prucher, Otto,16,
Puiforcat, Jean, 104, 105, 138

Rittweger, Otto, 95
Religous, *60, 61, 132*
Roccoco, 82
Rohde, Johan, 131
Rosenthal, Rena, 67, 69,
Rössiger, Wolfgang, 95
Ruhlman, 107

Schenk, Edouard, 105
Schweizer, Louis, 81, 82
Schweizer, Friedrich, 81, 82
Smoking accessories, *17, 20, 63, 64, 65, 75, 76-80,*
   92, 93, 95, 98, 133
Sporting motif, *40,54,58*
Staub, Daniel,.81, 82
Strnad, Oscar, 31, 32
Subes, Raymond, 104, 105
Sue' et Marie, 104, 105. 138
Szabo, Adalbert,105

Tableware, *11, 46, 82-91, 93, 94, 95, 97-99, 105,*
   120, 121, 122, 124, 125, 129, 130
Tümpel, Wolfgang, 95

Urban, Josef, 12

Vase, *12,14.48,88,89,118*
Vienna (Wiener)Secession, 9, 10

Wagdenfeld, Wilhelm, 95
Wärndorfer, Frits, 10
Warriors, *1,34-38,71,72,73*
Werbel and Czokally, 15
Wiener Keramics, 12
Wiener Werstätte, 5, 7, 10, 11, 12, 14, 16, 31, 78,
   105, 138
WMF, 5, 81, 82, 91, 138

Zach, Bruno,14
Zodiac, 77